P9-CKC-553

THE OBLIGATIONS OF POWER

Withdrawn by
Whitman College Library

The Obligations of Power

* AMERICAN DIPLOMACY IN THE SEARCH FOR PEACE

by Harlan Cleveland

Harper & Row, Publishers

NEW YORK AND LONDON

The quotation preceding the text, from *Times Three* by Phyllis McGinley, copyright 1953 by Phyllis McGinley, is reprinted by permission of The Viking Press, Inc.

E
840
.C6

THE OBLIGATIONS OF POWER. *Copyright © 1966 by Harlan Cleveland. Printed in the United States of America. All rights reserved. No part of this book may be used or reproduced in any manner whatsoever without written permission except in the case of brief quotations embodied in critical articles and reviews. For information address Harper & Row, Publishers, Incorporated, 49 East 33rd Street, New York, N. Y. 10016.*

FIRST EDITION

LIBRARY OF CONGRESS CATALOG CARD NUMBER: 66-13916

D-Q

For Lois

JUL 12 '66 Abel, Muse. budget, 1155

117993

Contents

Preface

A few days before this book was finished, I had to make a speech at one of those dinners where they don't care so much what you say, but do hope you will be on time. I was then working in the State Department in Washington and I asked my colleagues what they thought I ought to say about American foreign policy.

One of them said something like this:

"Sometimes I wonder if it is worth the effort to talk about foreign policy at all. Here I am, in the Department of State. In my family most of our conversation is about world affairs. My oldest son has a degree in international relations, is just back from two years in Vietnam, and is taking graduate work in Asian studies.

"Last evening he picked me up at the office to drive me home. He was discussing in great detail some paper he is working on about Indian foreign policy. My attention must have wandered a bit but suddenly I heard him say: 'By the way, Dad, what is our foreign policy?'"

I asked my friend, gently, what his answer had been.

He said, "By this time we were parking in front of the house. I told him that U. S. foreign policy was to try and create a workable system of world order—and let it go at that. What else could I do? It would have taken me all evening to explain how you do *that*."

Whether you have bought or borrowed this book, I am bound to assume that you have an evening to spend on it—and the book can easily be read in an evening. So I am going to talk to you quite informally about my current profession, which is to help build a workable world order.

It is not easy, I find, for a practitioner of diplomacy to write a book. We deal professionally with painful and contentious issues that touch the aspirations for which men fight and die, and with disputes on which governments rise and fall. Most international troubles yield, if at all, only to prolonged private exploration and necessarily quiet diplomacy. A diplomat, as Harold Nicholson once remarked, often has to choose between committing an indiscretion and uttering a cliché.

Yet there is still a wide area of interest that lies between the shocking and the soporific.

If the language of diplomatic discourse is sometimes bland, the issues are not. If the pursuit of foreign policy is quiet work, the purpose of foreign policy is the public business. And there is nothing mysterious about it—or so I will argue in these pages.

The object of American foreign policy is to place our power in the service of a world of diversity. We really believe, after 190 years, in our own Declaration of Independence, and we still think the philosophy it contains is good (as the Declaration itself declares) for "all Men."

We do not believe any one race or nation should own or manage the world. Indeed, we think the governance of our world of diversity is beyond the conception or the power or the skill of any one group, however talented. We foresee a "world order" with many centers of power, many places where important decisions are made, many international agencies of peaceful change, many devices for international conciliation, many checks and balances to prevent world order from becoming world dominion.

We try to hasten the advent of this kind of world order in two rather obvious ways: by trying to contain violence, and by inventing international means to deal with hundreds of common interests shared by few or many nations. Most of this work takes place behind the headlines, not because it is secret, and certainly not because it is uninteresting or unimportant, but because when we are successful there is no public conflict and therefore, by journalistic tradition, no news.

This double task, of keeping the peace and building the institutions of peaceful change, can best be understood by looking at it as the President of the United States has to look at it. Nobody but the President—not even his closest associates—can really feel the weight of final decisions about peace and war. But as citizens, you and I can at least approach each foreign policy question as though we had to come up with the answer. For citizen or for Presidential adviser, to be "responsible" means to confront honestly the self-query: "How would I do it, if I had it to do?"

This is the question that each Presidential adviser and the cluster of advisers to each adviser must ask themselves as the process of government goes on from day to day. For government is just a series of big and little private decisions by individual public servants.

Our mythology, of course, holds otherwise. Mythology holds that large public bureaucracies like the Department of State are depersonalized, that the decisions which emerge from them are the bloodless products of faceless men, camouflaged in equivocation and announced by disembodied spokesmen. But the men and women behind the myth are intensely human. They are working, they know, on matters of life and death. They are uncomfortably aware that the complexity of the questions they face makes the simple answer nearly always wrong. The decisions they make, the advice they give to the President, are not determined by pure logic or blind forces, but are ripped from the human conscience of sovereign individuals like you and me.

For several years I have been privileged to watch the management of U.S. foreign policy from close at hand, as ringside spectator and bit player in the drama of our destiny. From where I have been sitting I cannot see what the President sees, or feel what he feels. I have had frequent occasion, though, to ask myself what I would do if I had it to do—that is, to play an imaginary game of Presidential responsibility. This book is for people who also like to play that game.

I have been guided in its writing by a familiar, if usually unstated, author's ethic: It isn't plagiarism if you steal from yourself. Portions of this book have previously appeared in ephemeral forms, some (speeches) more ephemeral than others (articles in *Foreign Affairs*). Taken as a whole, it is suggested as an up-to-date way for American citizens to think about the use of American power in a world of disorder and diversity.

Since I have been working in a large organization, my thinking on foreign policy is bound to be something of a collective product. Nor can I readily trace to their sources all the ideas and concepts and formulations it contains. Some of them, I suppose, are original with me. Some are the result of having watched from a few blocks away, with professional interest and personal admiration, two extraordinary men, President Kennedy and President Johnson, fill to the brim the world's largest job. Some should in honesty be credited to officials with whom I have worked at various times in government: to Paul Hoffman and Averell Harriman, to Dean Rusk and Adlai Stevenson, to George Ball and McGeorge Bundy. Many of these ideas, perhaps most, originated with one or another of a remarkable group of colleagues with whom I have worked for more than four years in the State Department's Bureau of International Organization Affairs: notably Richard N. Gardner, Elmore Jackson, Walter Kotschnig, William B. Buffum, and Joseph J. Sisco, who succeeded me as Assistant Secretary of State for International Organization Affairs. In preparing the manuscript I had the help, beyond the call of duty, of Paul Phillips, and the technical aid and cheerful prodding of my secretary, Teresa Beach.

But the most obvious credit line is owing to Thomas W. Wilson, who is either a writer with a flair for policy making or a policy maker with a flair for writing—I never have quite decided which. Since 1961, Tom Wilson and I have collaborated so intimately on so many kinds of writing, and have edited each other's copy so mercilessly, that I find it no longer possible to remember which twists of thought or turns of phrase are his and which are mine. His modesty precludes my listing him on the title page; thus I may only mention here, with gratitude and affection, his enormous creative contribution to our common way of thinking about the obligations of power.

Paris, France
September 20, 1965

HARLAN CLEVELAND

"Rejoice that under cloud and star
    The planet's more than Maine or Texas.
Bless the delightful fact there are
    Twelve months, nine muses, and two sexes;
And infinite in earth's dominions
    Arts, climates, wonders and opinions."
—PHYLLIS McGINLEY, *In Praise of Diversity*

THE OBLIGATIONS OF POWER

The Spirit We Are Of

1

In the cold air of an October night in 1962, at the height of the Cuba missile crisis, a crowd of pickets appeared in front of the White House with grim faces and freshly painted signs. The District of Columbia police, who are fairly perceptive about these matters, carefully separated the pickets into two groups, according to the legends on their placards. One band of marchers demonstrated against the use of force in the crisis; the other opposed the use of diplomacy.

Inside the bustling, brightly lit White House the President of the United States was studying all the ways of combining force and diplomacy to get those missiles out of Cuba without a nuclear war. Making my way into a White House meeting that night, I wondered if any of the marchers could imagine how complex a task that was—and how important to every man, woman, and child on earth.

The most important single factor in world affairs is not what happens in Moscow or London, in Paris or Peking. It is how the government and people of the United States of America, the world's oldest and liveliest democracy, decide to combine their force and their diplomacy to serve their interests. The interests of the United States are global, and that is good fortune for all the world's peoples and most of their leaders. For in a hundred political crises and a thousand technical fields, the American people and their government have decided to use their enormous power in the service of diversity.

The goals of our foreign policy are certainly unique for a leading world power. Through the ages of man, the foreign policies of great powers have been designed principally to serve the goals of national expansion, that is, to build empire and then to defend it against rival empires or, more recently, against revolts by subject peoples.

This was true, in various ways and varying degrees, of the ancient empires in Asia and the Middle East and the Mediterranean. It was true of the European empires of the seventeenth and eighteenth centuries—and of the Russian czars as well. Mussolini's goal was to re-establish a Roman empire; Hitler's goal was dominion from the Atlantic to the Persian Gulf; Stalin's goal was to re-establish the Russian empire as a base for a communist world. Even the British, who brought us up and loosed us on an unsuspecting world, through most of their history tested their actions by the interests of empire.

Now it was one thing to fashion a foreign policy to further the aims of territorial expansion and colonial rule. Since the aims were primitive, the policies and techniques could be primitive, too. They could be explained with simple slogans, measured by square miles on colored maps, and celebrated by reminders of great victories on bloody fields of battle.

But our policy is the opposite of empire. It is, as President Kennedy used to say, to make the world safe for diversity. We do not seek to expand our territory, or rule other peoples, or control resources beyond our frontiers. We are not engaged in a holy war to force other people to accept our kind of government or conform to our way of life.

Our purposes in the world are different because our experience at home has been different, and that is the nub of it. "When will people learn," Macaulay asked, "that it is the spirit we are of, not the machinery we employ, that binds us to others?"

It is no special credit to us that we pursue a foreign policy matched to our own national experience. To believe in diversity should not be difficult for an American. As we look around our own nation and the world, it is not easy to believe in anything else.

In this world there are a good many nations, and countless parties and organizations, that passionately believe some single national state, some unifying political doctrine, some monochromatic race of men, can and should dominate the world. But we Americans know that nations are too independent, doctrines too changeable, and individuals just too ornery to give these claims and pretensions much of a chance in the real world. We know these things not because we have figured them out rationally, but because that is the kind of people we are, and diversity is where we came from.

Ever since our forefathers were carried away by their heady ideas about the dignity of the human person and the unalienable rights of men born equal, the basic direction of our foreign policy has been preordained. The notions we work with in dealing with other countries are quite directly the product of our own successful experiments with government by consent of the governed, with trial by jury and the rule of law.

The racial and ethnic and national groups that came here, and read a sign in the harbor saying, "Send these, the homeless, tempest-tost, to me," have not had an easy time making diversity work. We like to think of our nation as a great melting pot, but our history betrays our self-image. The peoples who came to America cleaved to each other in enduring cultural groups, for bargaining with the other groups that had already come and for protection against those further waves of strangers that kept rolling in past the Statue of Liberty and populating a continent with a nation of foreigners.

The new Americans and the older Americans learned in time to tolerate each other—which did not at all mean they had to *like* each other, just that they agreed not to judge each other by their own lights. As they rubbed up against one another, they discovered not merely that all men are brothers—that was an earlier, easier lesson—but that all brothers are different, which is a later, harder lesson because it means learning about the value of difference.

Of course, in our earlier days we set a limit to tolerance. If foreigners wanted to be tolerated, there was a fixed requirement: They had to want to be Americans.

Then when we started going to Europe as tourists and traders, we had to make a special effort to remember we were moving among the people whose ancestors did *not* want to come to America. And now, as Americans by the hundreds of thousands move around in Africa and Asia and Latin America, we have to learn once again that toughest of elementary lessons, the value of difference.

Even as we learn the lesson, it is not easy to articulate it. Visitors to the United States usually find us more than a little confusing—so busy arguing among ourselves on how to fulfill the promises of our forefathers that we can hardly spare the time to argue with our visitors. When we do, we find that many of them come from societies which describe their goals and define their "system" with practiced words from ancient manuscripts and modern manifestoes.

We do not, of course, have a "system." We have a protected plurality of systems. Edmund Burke, in his famous speech about how to get along with those wild men across the Atlantic, said in despair that our religion was "the dissidence of dissent." Americans, Burke thought, were "a people who are still, as it were, but in the gristle, and not yet hardened into the bone of manhood."

But in the 190 years since that speech we have learned, from hardening, bone-building experience in peace and war, that the best and most durable way to manage our public business is the undogmatic, unsystematic, loose-reined, checked-and-balanced government called democracy. We have learned to distrust the idea that any one man's view of society, or any one group's view of society, is the correct, approved, authorized version. The one essential thing about democracy, I suppose, is this: that no individual or group ever gains the exclusive right to say, with authority, what democracy is.

"A charming form of government," Plato wryly called it, "full of variety and disorder, dispensing a sort of equality to equals and unequals alike."

We have successfully advertised this preference of ours for pluralism—and our pretension that freedom is good for everybody. We advertised them in our Declaration of Independence, in our Constitution, in acts of our Congress, in decisions of our courts, and in Presidential words and deeds that have touched every continent and infected every people with the contagious virus of freedom.

We have not always done justice to the values we served with our lips. But there is no doubt that the great built-in advantage of our foreign policy is that, by and large, we really mean what we say about the dignity of man and the independence of nations. The philosophy of our Declaration has been rewritten in six official languages now, as a guide for all men everywhere, in the preamble and the first two articles of the United Nations Charter. Most people in all countries, however governed, share our goals and seek them as their own, for they spring from aspirations deeply rooted in human nature. And that is why we find so many people are willing to cooperate with us so often on so many different matters.

Our foreign policy, then, can best be seen as an effort to carry into world affairs what we have learned, here at home, about how men and women of different nations and different regions, men and women who treasure different kinds of heritages and different ideas about God and politics, can live their lives and pursue their personal goals without murdering each other.

The world in which we try to support these precepts with our power is increasingly diverse—gloriously, irretrievably diverse—diverse in social organization, in economic theories, in political ideas; diverse in attitudes and alliances, in wealth and power; diverse, too, in the stages of economic growth.

In such a world, we want above all to be sure that no nation or group of nations ever gains the exclusive right even to define world order, let alone to manage it. And in this respect, at least, most of the world's peoples seem to agree with us.

Fifteen years ago, there were clearly two poles, two centers of world power, with allies and satellites clustered around them for protection. Now the diffusion of relevant power is already well advanced.

Western Europe is back on its feet—and acting like it. Throughout the free world, middle-sized nations and groupings of smaller states are asserting their right to think differently from the great powers, elbowing their way into world politics, insisting that *their* border troubles, their terms of trade, their sense of racial wrongs and human rights, and their U.N. votes all be weighed and counted in the computations of current history. And in that once monolithic bloc of communist nations, the Yugoslavs have managed to maintain their independence for a decade and a half, the Eastern European satellites are pulling away from the Moscow sun, and the Chinese and the Russians are talking about each other in almost unbelievably offensive language.

As the din gets louder and the shouters more numerous, our problem is to keep clearly in mind that most of these developments are right down the middle of the road to the world we want to live in. A multipolar world of independent nations—a world of protected variety—would constitute the safest environment for our own kind of society.

If the goals of diversity with safety are without precedent in history, so also is the scale of the power available to pursue them. We will soon have an economy that turns out the unimaginable sum of one trillion dollars' worth of goods and services in a year's time. The constructive capacity of our science and technology is already growing faster than we can build the institutions to channel and control it. As for our destructive power, we are numbed by repetition of its scale.

It is easy to remember that a single warhead now can pack more destructive wallop than all the explosives used in World War II. Such power in the hands of two nations, each capable of delivering it to the other's doorstep, was almost bound to produce a stalemate and focus the eyes of responsible leaders on its limitation rather than its use.

When destructive power grows past the point where it can be used without self-destruction, the conventional military wisdom that has instructed generals and statesmen through the ages is suddenly obsolescent; most of the remaining questions are not military but political. President Kennedy, who during his first summer in office spoke of disarmament as "a propaganda thing," did his homework on the simultaneous equations of survival and concluded that "in the long run, the only real security in this age of nuclear power rests not in armament but in disarmament." "Our foremost aim," he also said, "is the control of force, not the pursuit of force, in a world made safe for mankind."

A hard look at all the secrets of nuclear weaponry makes each occupant of the White House acutely, soberly, almost painfully aware of the restraint which responsible management of such power imposes on a President of the United States. "There is no alternative to peace," said President Eisenhower. Shortly after the Cuba missile crisis, President Kennedy wrote the moral to the story in a memorable sentence: "Above all, while defending our own vital interests, nuclear powers must avert those confrontations which bring an adversary to a choice of either a humiliating retreat or a nuclear war." And in the first foreign policy declaration of his

Presidency, Lyndon B. Johnson showed that he thoroughly understood the care with which his suddenly awesome power would have to be used:

> In this age where there can be no losers in peace and no victors in war—we must recognize the obligation to match national strength with national restraint . . .

As the world's most powerful nation, then, we must also be the world's most responsible nation. The paradox of using power in the service of diversity is this: We are so strong that we cannot do much of anything by ourselves any more.

A World of Small Wars

2

What makes diversity work, as we have found here at home, is not men's ability to agree on philosophy or broad principles, but their ability to agree on what to do next, while continuing to disagree as to why they are doing it.

Some may agree to take the "next step" for gain or greed or glory, which is to say that their interests are served thereby; others may see a mandate for the same "next step" in some ancient religious scroll or nineteenth century economics textbook; still others may go along because they don't want to offend those who are proposing that the step be taken. The reasons for common action can be mutually inconsistent. I think they often are in any large organization, and in international relations almost always.

In the North Atlantic alliance, each of fifteen allies has its own interests and its own concept of the proper way to defend Western Europe; yet they more or less cooperate in spending $30 billion for the defense of Europe each year. If, in the United Nations, we had to wait around until two-thirds of the delegates who meet in the General Assembly could agree as to why they were agreeing, no action resolution would ever be passed and the United Nations would not today be spending more than $500 million a year for peace-keeping and nation-building.

What unites our diversity, then, is not so much a paper agreement on philosophy as a many-splendored consensus on procedure, a variety of pragmatic agreements as to how decisions will be made and who will carry them into action. It is no accident that the Charter of the United Nations contains five pages of philosophy followed by fifty pages of procedure.

The question, of course, is not whether we agree with the philosophy. That is easy. The difficult question is how we get there from where we have to start—which is here, and today.

"Here" is a world of international ironies.

It is a world with 20 million men under arms and annual military budgets of $120 billion—which has trouble finding 20,000 men and $120 million for international peace-keeping by the United Nations.

It is a world in which the big powers urge the smaller powers to stay away from nuclear weapons, yet feel they have to build their own nuclear stockpiles for their own national purposes, or for the common defense.

It is a world in which the small nations complain that the nuclear powers are not getting on with disarmament, while they themselves negotiate for the best deal in a squadron of jet fighters or a package of secondhand howitzers and flame throwers.

It is a world that never leaves us alone. When he first came into office, Secretary of State Dean Rusk used to point out that the sun never set on scenes of trouble; at any moment in the twenty-four hour cycle, there was plenty of light for a good riot somewhere in the world. My own observation is that peace and security crises are generally timed for Friday night or Saturday morning, Washington time—and last just long enough to ruin the weekends of the responsible officials in the world's chancelleries.

And it is a world where no breach of the peace escapes the

notice of the United States. In the age of ultimate weapons, those who possess them must measure each local dispute by its potential for escalation to general war. The price of power is involvement. Paraguay and Nepal do not have to watch the cables and the tickers for signs of violence, because they do not have the wherewithal to do something about it. For better or worse, we do.

The fact that our power gives us some responsibility for peace everywhere seems to bother a good many Americans.

Some of these critics have never quite gotten used to a world in which most of the problems are outside of Europe. They were used to having to worry about Alsace-Lorraine or even the Polish frontier. But to be told that we also have to concern ourselves with the Chaco, the Congo, and the Rann of Kutch—that is too much.

It is fortunately true that in Europe, scene of most of the wars featured in our ethnocentric history books, fewer people are killing each other today than at any time since Charlemagne. Even in Europe the Greeks and Turks are glaring at each other over Cyprus; every European nation is armed to the teeth; and the Wall, with what it portends, still makes Berlin the world's most dangerous trouble spot. But in recent years the headlines have been full of crises in the rest of the world.

We are not permitted for more than a few days at a time to ignore the raw conflicts among the new states of Africa, where the Somalis and the Ethiopians argue over an arid but precious piece of no man's land, the Algerians and Moroccans dispute a wedge of oily sand in the Sahara, and the Congo is periodically attacked by teen-age gangs led and equipped by other African nations. In southern Africa, racial strife reminds us of much unfinished business—African nationalists filter back to Angola with new arms and fresh determination, Rhodesia's rebellion threatens to bring on new racial warfare, and South Africa courts bloodshed and disaster with its policy of racial separation.

Nor does Asia allow us to forget that it is the biggest continent, and has long been the most turbulent as well. Israel and its Arab neighbors still face each other in unliquidated war. A fratricidal feud mars the beauty of the incomparable Vale of Kashmir—and has recently enlivened much of the long India-Pakistan frontier. In India itself, men prepare against another attack from Communist China; and north of China, even the Russians complain of hundreds of border violations by the Chinese. Guerrillas disturb the peace in Borneo, and Indonesian leaders talk of crushing their northern neighbor, Malaysia.

In the Far East the settled ambitions of a new breed of Communists encounter the growing resistance of those who must decide —because they can do something about it—whether the Chinese Communists and their friends will be contained sooner, or will have to be stopped later elsewhere. Endemic violence has become acute and international in Vietnam. New violence erupts from time to time onto the Plain of Jars in Laos. In the Straits of Formosa, the Chinese periodically renew their shelling of the island of Quemoy, steppingstone to Taiwan—but have left it at that for a decade in deference to the U.S. Seventh Fleet. And on that lonely and forgotten front, the 38th parallel in Korea, American sentries are still subject to ambush by Communist infiltrators.

In the Western Hemisphere, Castro's Cuba keeps festering, exporting trouble to Venezuela and elsewhere. Real economic progress, especially in the big ABC countries of South America, is still offset by the cycle of revolt and repression in several other countries which have developed more nationalism than nationhood. In the Dominican Republic, OAS peace-keepers had to force a halt to mounting violence and armed anarchy.

All these tangled and troubled disputes, these eruptions on the world's thin political skin, are merely the inventory in 1965, as this is written. In another few months, when the book is published, we may well be nursing other crises in parts of the world now apparently quiescent. But many of the raw spots I have mentioned are hardy perennials, and some of these running sores will still be open and bleeding whenever you may read these words. Look around the world as you read, and see.

Why is the world so unsettled and unsettling, so noisy and so importunate? Why is there suddenly, in our time, so much ugly, small-scale trouble in the world? The answer is obvious: We are living through the growing pains of diversity.

In the old imperial system, each big nation took care of keeping the peace within its own "sphere of influence"—a state of affairs for which the Chinese Communists and some American commentators betray a certain nostalgia. There might be big wars among the big powers, but little wars and local massacres were readily suppressed or limited to local effects by these same big powers. They had both the strength and (they assumed) the mandate to reach out a large and sometimes clumsy paw to discourage undue resort to violence among the weaker tribes and principalities in their respective domains. They made, in short, all the "peace-keeping" decisions.

The system of empire and spheres of influence broke up fast after World War II. But the violent consequences of diversity were not immediately apparent. This was partly because most of the imperial powers were convinced that dependent peoples would get their independence sooner or later, and contrived to make it sooner. Only in Indochina and Algeria, where the French resisted the inevitable, and in the Indian subcontinent, where communal bitterness overflowed at the moment of partition, did the decolonization of nearly one billion people give rise to much killing.

As the great empires were dismembered, local and regional wars were held in check by a new fear, the fear that any local war might quickly become a nuclear war. But then came the thermonuclear stalemate, advertised by the quick defusing of the Cuba missile crisis of 1962, dramatized the following year by the test ban treaty and the unanimous U.N. resolution against placing weapons of mass destruction in orbit in outer space.

Thus, just as the world began to hope it would not die of a nuclear thrombosis, it suddenly seemed to break out with the measles. By the autumn of 1965 there were 49 active border disputes—one for every two significant sovereignties in the world. Ancient resentments and modern rivalries now create the big black headlines and activate the small black cars that shuttle experts back and forth between the State Department and the White House, at hours determined by angry men with homemade weapons in some remote corner of the world. (I remember one emergency call from the State Department's Operations Center, which awakened me with the news that a Congolese government airplane had been shot down in Kivu Province by a teen-age guerrilla with a bow and arrow.)

And behind the contrived riots and the native revolts too well equipped to be native, a larger, grimmer competition shows through the indigenous facades—competition between those who think their interests will thrive on chaos and bloodshed and those who, like us, think their interests lie in keeping change peaceful.

The alternative to world war, it seems, is not world peace. It is a world full of small wars and rumors of wars.

All this is most distressing, to be sure. But do we Americans have to be so heavily involved in it?

We were all brought up on John Donne: "No man is an Island, intire of itselfe . . . any man's death diminishes me, because I am involved in Mankinde." But still, do we have to have our Attorney General in Djakarta, our Undersecretary of State in Cyprus, our Ambassador to the United Nations mediating a Kashmir debate, and our Secretary of Defense in Vietnam, all in the very same winter? Do we really have to be so very much involved, in so many ugly grudge fights, in so many places, with so many different varieties of "Mankinde"?

The answer is "yes." Because we do not want to have to use our ultimate power, we must constantly be using more limited forms of power, serving (sometimes without being invited) as the world's leading peacemakers and peace-keepers.

We are involved because we are too large and powerful to hide. Sometimes we forget how big we really are. Look at it this way: In the three years 1961–1962–1963—roughly, the three years of the Kennedy Administration—our gross national product went up from $500 billion to $600 billion a year. That increase, the increment of $100 billion, was more than the total combined gross national product of 84 members of the United Nations, including nearly all the countries whose frontier disputes and internal struggles for power are creating the headline crises of our time.

If we often seem to be in the middle of these crises, it is not because we are often direct parties at interest. Usually we are not promoting the interests of one rival against another—in Kashmir, for example, or in the continuing troubles between Israel and its Arab neighbors. We are, instead, partisans of peaceful procedures; our national interest is to see to it that disputes do not lead to violence and violence to war. But power is exercised from the middle of a problem, not from the sidelines, and that is why we are generally in the middle.

We are concerned about every breach of the peace because the peace of the world is all too likely to prove indivisible, and because if trouble spreads, local Communists backed by major Communist powers have an opportunity to take sides as a prelude to taking over. We are involved because we are widely believed to have the power to fight or prevent fighting, to sit on the lid or let the pot boil over, to change or maintain the existing balance of political power in nearly every part of the globe. And this impression is not far from the truth. For we are probably the only nation which now has the wealth, firepower, airlift capacity, organizational skill, and (we hope) political imagination to put together an operational world system for peaceful change.

Granting that the residual capacity for dealing with conflict and containing violence rests with the armed forces of the United

States, does that mean we have to be the world's policeman, all by ourselves?

This time the answer is "no."

We do not have to be the world's policeman *if* we have the wit and skill to work with other nations in building international peace-keeping machinery instead. This is why we have worked with 42 allies to build an interlocking matrix of commonwealths in the Western Hemisphere, in the North Atlantic, in the Far East and Southeast Asia. This is why we work so hard to build a workable United Nations.

If, in the primitive state of international peace-keeping machinery, we sometimes seem to be carrying the lion's share of the peace-keeping load, put it down to the fact that in the jungle of world politics we are now the lion. Some few Americans may still prefer some other world role—that of a mouse or a parrot or an ostrich, perhaps. But it seems that most Americans, given the choice, would rather lead than follow, would rather use our enormous power to build the kind of world we want to live in, rather than let somebody else take the responsibility for building world peace with less room for diversity.

Our problem is to get accustomed to our own power, and to the implications of its global availability. Too many Americans are still reluctant and plaintive about the policeman's lot. We know from hard and recent experience, as well as from Gilbert and Sullivan, that it is not a happy one. But we also know that it is an essential function of civilized society and that it can be shared with others if we work hard enough at sharing it.

In a troubled world the Beatitudes get scrambled. Cursed are the peacemakers: for they shall be called just about every name there is *except* the children of God. The hallmark of our national maturity will be a citizenry which knows that power and popularity seldom come in the same package.

The Agony of Success

3

For the citizens of a great nation engaged in global peacemaking, a sense of weary frustration is never far below the surface of public consciousness. Small wonder. Our dedication to diversity requires our getting used to an extraordinary series of ideas:

• We want other countries to be independent, and peoples to be free to make their own choices, including their own mistakes.

• Unlike most other nations and peoples, we have the power to do something about it.

• Doing something about world order means getting involved, one way or another, in the affairs of every nation on earth— whether their current leaders relish our leadership or not, whether their newspapers and radio commentators praise us for it or not.

• The best techniques of leadership are those which widen the community of people who feel responsible for action, building organizations in which smaller nations can cooperate with us in a relationship of dignity and seeming equality.

• Therefore, the more successful we are in achieving our foreign policy goals, the more we will be involved with other nations and the more independent—of *us*—those other nations will feel and act.

The operation of United States foreign policy therefore generates a chronic low-grade fever in our own body politic, induced by acute annoyance and marked by the familiar symptoms of anxiety —prophecies of doom, doubts about our capacity to lead, certainty that other peoples are somehow better at this sort of thing than Americans are—all expressed in a fearful, angry, or indignant tone of voice.

No symptomatic relief, buffered or otherwise, will help. The frustrations are not apparent, but real. They are, indeed, the product of the past successes of our foreign policies. For success does make life more complicated.

I would not know from personal experience what happens when a man succeeds in amassing a million dollars, but I have the impression that it increases both his personal problems and his social complications.

Certainly when a man succeeds in reaching a higher position in his organization or profession, he is promptly rewarded with harder work, greater controversy, and tougher decisions than he had to make before. When a candidate for public office succeeds at the polls, he wins, in return for his trouble, a bigger bucket of more complex trouble.

And any man who has won an affirmative answer to a proposal of marriage knows what complexity flows from that success.

Some people think that world affairs ought to be different. The solution of any problem, they feel, should reduce by one the number of problems remaining to be solved. They assume that success in achieving some aim of foreign policy today should make international life that much easier and simpler tomorrow. Yet the plain fact is that in international politics the success of past and present policies can make life tomorrow quite a bit more frustrating than it was yesterday.

Consider as an example the success of Woodrow Wilson's notion (it was Jefferson's, too) that our national policy is to promote the self-determination of peoples. We were the original anti-colonialists, and in half a century we have helped more than half a hundred peoples to achieve their national independence.

But now they are much less comfortable to live with, precisely because they are more independent of our leadership than they were before. They now hold nearly half the votes in the General Assembly of the United Nations, and have converted that organization into something very different from—though not, I will later argue, less valuable to us than—the United Nations in which we used to have things mostly our own way. To preach diversity is one thing; to have it preached at us, as criticism of NATO or justification for more U.S. aid, is a different experience.

Take as another example what is now accepted as a brilliant foreign policy success: the Marshall Plan for European recovery. Our aim was to enable Europe to get back its economic health; the Europeans with our help succeeded beyond the dreams of those who laid the original plans for that extraordinary enterprise.

A few years ago one of our weekly news magazines (which had opposed the Marshall Plan) came out with an article emblazoned on its front cover as "The World's Greatest Success Story—Now It Can Be Told." The "world's greatest success story" turned out to be the story of the Marshall Plan. And "now it can be told" is one formula by which an editor can admit an earlier error. Yet the main burden of the article was a bitter complaint that the Marshall Plan was such a success that Europe had become *too* healthy. The Europeans, the article protested, were competing aggressively for export markets and forcing American industry to get up early in the morning to stay in the game.

That is not even half the price we are paying for the success of our postwar policy in Europe. The European nations now stand on their own feet, look us straight in the eye, and bargain with us hard on tariff rates and money matters. The Europeans even feel strong enough to want a larger voice in the military defense of Europe. This is what we wanted all along, because self-reliant allies were, in fact, the only realistic alternative to a Communist takeover in the late forties. But the success of our policy certainly has made life in the Atlantic community more complicated—and, for the time being, more frustrating.

As in our personal lives, therefore, success in solving one problem leads to deeper involvement in efforts to solve more complex problems. One thing not only leads to another; in the politics of diversity, it generally leads to several others.

The tone of anger and frustration that marks our foreign policy debates is partly the price we pay for freedom. What most Americans think about foreign policy is not what they are told to think, either by the government or by the men and women who write editorials or ghostwrite commentaries for radio and TV personalities. We make up our collective mind on the basis of "the facts." The question is, what facts are coming our way from day to day?

Nobody expects reporting and editing by a free press to be an exercise in pristine objectivity. Everybody knows that, in Max Ascoli's phrase, all facts are not born equal, with an inalienable right to be heard. The news service reporter who writes or dictates a story sets in train a selection and screening process which is continued by the wire service editors, then at relay points, and later still by the editors of a newspaper. The average daily newspaper finally prints perhaps one-quarter of the copy carried on the main trunk of the news service. In the process, half a dozen judgments may be made as to whether a given event is news in the first place, what aspect of the event is most newsworthy, what else has to be said to tell the whole story, how much of the story is worth passing on, what prominence it rates under what kind of head, and, finally, whether it is worth printing at all in some of the precious space available.

Only a few stories survive this daily multiple-choice examination. They are selected for publication because they mean something to each of the selectors along the route, or at least have to do with people whose names each of the selectors can recognize. Even among the stories that pass these tests, many fall by the wayside because of practices that have seemed acceptable, even "professional," for long enough to be taught as traditions of the trade by schools of journalism. Somehow the net result is a flat, one-dimensional quality to most of the international news that finally reaches our eyes and ears as *"the* news."

Some of the offending "traditions" represent no more than the lazy acceptance of conventional lines of least resistance. These operate in journalism the way Gresham's law does in monetary affairs—for technical reasons the bad drives out the good. There is the Law that local news displaces national or international news. There is the Law that early, "budgeted" news happening in predictable places pushes out late-breaking, hard-to-get news happening in areas that have not been carefully arranged for ahead of time. And there is something close to a Law that any old speech mimeographed in advance pushes out what the speaker actually says when he gets to the podium, because the reporter has already written his story and gone to dinner.

Another "tradition" that flattens perspective is the doctrine that only what happened yesterday is news today; or, in news magazines, that the writer must peg whatever he wants to report on something that happened last week. Most really important events go on for months or years. To take them at the flood, to pinpoint the day of decision and destiny, is not easy; it is practically impossible for those who run as they write. The compulsion to fix an event at a point in time, forgetting its past and failing to foresee its future, diminishes the dynamism and continuity and interrelatedness which are close to the essence of human affairs.

Another technical factor that contributes to superficiality is that the task of reporting important events must often be done in a matter of hours, or, for the wire services, sometimes in minutes. This does confront the writer and editor with a serious problem; but a public official engaged in making some of that news can only say in mock sympathy, "Welcome to the club." Public officials frequently have to assemble facts, arrive at complex judgments, and take action within a few days or a few hours, or less. Most of the same facts and considerations are usually available to the reporters, and for very nearly as long. If the reporter has a full day, as he often does, to work on a single important story, that is a luxury of time and concentration not usually available even to an Assistant Secretary of State, much less to a Secretary of State or a President. In short, journalists are likely to have as much time to pull together all the pieces that give depth and balance to a story as the newsmakers have to do what is reported in the story. It is not impossible to do a first-rate job of work under these conditions; the proof is that some writers consistently do so.

Not long before he was deposed, Nikita Khrushchev was badgered by a group of reporters about their difficulties in getting hard news about Soviet policy. "Any damn fool could learn to be a journalist," he said with a tolerant smile, "if the job were not so difficult."

The technical difficulties of the journalistic profession are troublesome enough. But the most damage to public understanding of American foreign policy is done by wide acceptance in the profession of the following propositions:

1. That good news is no news;
2. That bad news sells newspapers;
3. That a prediction of imminent disaster is better copy than a report of constructive action to avoid disaster.

To most public officials, the public press seems caught up in a macabre syndrome of conflict, hatred, and violence. Paul Hoffman, who has spent much of his life administering large, constructive, public interest programs—and not getting adequate attention for them in the papers—tells of an apartment developer who complained to a New York editor about the lack of coverage of his building program. The editor gave him a frank and revealing reply: "Build the world's most modern skyscraper, and I'll give it a couple of paragraphs on the financial page. But dynamite the least modern two-story brownstone, and I'll get you a full column on page one."

An unbalanced daily diet of conflict, crisis, riot, and alarm in international affairs conveys the general impression that things are bad all over, that the world of freedom is in headlong retreat, that war is inevitable sooner or later, that our government is blundering into one morass after another, using clumsy tactics in support of a nebulous strategy. This impression is wrong, yet it is widely held. I have come to believe that the daily featuring of bad news and the daily neglect of good news does large and unnecessary damage to the U.S. national interest by inducing in segments of the American public an unwarranted mood of apocalyptic frustration.

This might not be so serious if we found on our front pages only the bad news that has already happened. But we find there also much bad news that has not happened yet and may not ever happen.

The men and women who practice journalism and those who practice diplomacy have much in common. Both groups deal in crises. But the journalists deal with more crises than the diplomats do. Despite the well-known pressures of time and space, the media of mass communication seem to find room not only for disasters that do occur but also for those that do not.

In 1961, when I began to deal professionally with United Nations affairs, most newspapers and many radio and TV commentators were absorbed in fascination with the Soviet proposal for a troika—a three-headed executive for the world organization, designed to give the Communists a veto over all U.N. executive actions, and aimed especially at the Congo operation which was interfering with the Soviet drive to establish a Communist military presence in Central Africa.

This administrative monstrosity was greeted with cries of alarm and despondency by headline writers and editorialists all over the United States, just as if it had a chance to be adopted. We knew— and anybody who studied the politics of the United Nations would know—that the troika never even left the starting line. When the Soviets finally counted noses in the General Assembly, they found only two countries in the whole world outside the little band of Soviet satellites that favored the troika proposal. Thereupon, without any public announcement, the Soviets dropped the idea, and it died, as it was always fated to die, with a whimper.

Looking through a number of newspapers the next day, including some that had earlier reported the Soviet threat in black headlines, I found only one newspaper in a large sample which even mentioned the death of the troika proposal at the time it died.

The enormous power of which the American nation now disposes, and our continuing conviction that it should be used in ways the American public at large endorses and ultimately directs, give our own myths and moods a special relevance in international relations. It is altogether fitting that in a great democracy at a critical time, the first problem of foreign policy should be domestic public opinion.

From this point of view, the greatest danger to world peace could be a rising mood of self-induced frustration in the United States of America, an attitude from which it might come to seem that there were only two exits: belligerence or defeatism.

Public moods are hard to measure and harder to explain. But one does not have to search far these days for one prime source of current frustration: a persistent, pervasive, and mistaken impression that the story of the Cold War is the story of one long, unbroken retreat by the West before the juggernaut of international communism guided by the master minds in the Kremlin.

One reason for this impression is the journalistic penchant for conflict and trouble which I have already discussed. The language in which world politics is described too often comes out of sportswriting—we always have to be "up" or "down," never merely working at a problem—or out of war reporting. For a decade or more there has been a vogue for a whole vocabulary of arresting if irrelevant analogies to describe the "war called peace," complete with its "fronts" and "weapons," "strategy" and "tactics," each "confrontation" or "battle" leading of course to "victory" or "defeat."

The recurring fear that all is lost would not, however, be stifled even if all journalists were as thoughtful and responsible as a good many prove to be. For the mood of frustration is induced partly by the prolific output of certain scholarly Kremlinologists who have become hypnotized by the Communist prophets they want us all to read. Because the Communists proclaim the inevitability of their victory, some experts would have us believe that there is a Master Plan for world conquest, and, what is more, that this Master Plan will work. The summary version of this view was contained in a single irrelevant photo caption that appeared in the undeniably anti-Communist *U.S. News & World Report* during 1961: "No matter which side wins, communism seems destined to gain in the end."

There are other, deeper, more subtle factors in American history, attitudes, and ways of thinking that may also be contributing to a mood of public frustration.

One is the traditional search for simple answers to complicated problems. Another is the approach which takes for granted that any "problem" must have a "solution." Still another is the conviction that there are two "sides" to any question. In our world, there is hardly an issue which has as few as two sides. For one week, at my desk in the State Department, I counted the identifiable "sides" to every question I had occasion to touch. For readers who are impressed by statistics, I will report that the average problem in my field, international organizations, had five and one half sides.

Yet two-sidedness is built deep into our culture and education, and is confirmed by our experience of sports events, college debating, two-party elections, and adversary proceedings in our courts. It encourages a value system which teaches that one side, or viewpoint, or doctrine, or policy is "right" and the other therefore "wrong"—leaving no room for mutually exclusive descriptions of the same phenomenon by different people, and no room for compromise and accommodation, which are the other names for politics. Khrushchev must have been lying, many people thought, when he spoke of West Berlin as a "cancer" or a "bone in his throat," because we knew perfectly well that it was a "showcase of freedom" and a "symbol of hope."

Whatever the reasons for a national mood of frustration and uncertainty, it has brought into being in recent years a vocal minority of Americans who seek office and ask for the voters' confidence on the spurious ground that the Communists are winning and we are losing. The irony is that this minority made its major appearance on the national scene just when two decades of bipartisan policy were beginning to show dramatic results.

Our aim, under four Presidents, has been to contain communism and to help build a strong, prosperous, diverse world of independent nations infected with the highly contagious virus of freedom. The performance is beginning to resemble the promise a little. The way to see this most clearly is to look out at the world for a moment from the Kremlin balcony. What is increasingly clear to us must be all too clear to the leaders of the Soviet Union.

First, they know that Karl Marx's "iron laws of history" do not seem to work very well. Capitalism turned out to be something more than a transitional stage from feudalism to socialism, and will evidently not collapse of its own internal contradictions. In an interview shortly before his political demise, Khrushchev described capitalism as one of several "established" systems. Marx must have stirred in his grave, but Khrushchev's successors do not seem to entertain any illusions about the imminent collapse of the United States.

Second, the Communist leaders have learned—the hard way—that they just cannot expand their empire beyond Stalin's gains by military aggression or military pressure. They learned that nuclear terror did not work, that propaganda does not blow down governments. The Communist parties outside the present Communist countries are generally weaker than they have been for twenty years. And although half a hundred new nations have been formed since World War II, not one of them has chosen communism as a way of life or a system of government. There is something very wrong with this picture, if you look at it from the Kremlin balcony.

Third, the Soviet leaders know now that the race to gain nuclear superiority, or even nuclear equality with the United States, can never be won, and may no longer be relevant anyhow. They know that nuclear war would inflict unacceptable damage on the Soviet Union; and, since our immediate reaction in the Korean and Cuban crises, they are cautious about conventional wars, too, fearing nuclear risks they do not want to take. They are having more success, they feel, with the indirect forms of aggression known as "wars of liberation," but even that technique is becoming dangerously risky, as the escalation in Vietnam has made clear.

Fourth, the leaders of world communism have had to relearn everything they learned in school about the economics of Marx. For the communist system has turned out to be a major disaster for agriculture everywhere in the Soviet bloc, with the partial exception of Poland where 87 per cent of the land is still privately farmed. The Soviet leaders—and worse, their farmers—have learned that you cannot farm with police power, but only with incentives. And they can see ahead a long and expensive task of trying to modernize Soviet agriculture to bring the rural slum half of the Soviet population into step with the industrial half.

In Eastern Europe the satellites are even experimenting with such ideas as incentive wages and interest on capital, and are reaching out for trade relations with Western Europe and the United States. When the Chinese Communists tried a great leap forward they stumbled because of communist agricultural economics. In Cuba, it took something over a million dollars a day of Soviet aid plus a rationing system and the secret police to offset the mess Castro made. The race to outproduce the Western economies has not been won by the communists, and they are embarrassingly aware of the fact.

Finally, the force of communist ideology no longer causes nations to work together—instead, it drives them apart. Brezhnev, Kosygin, Mao, Tito, Gomulka, and Castro all claim to be Communists, and all argue with each other about ideology.

Other Communist states are less and less inclined to take orders from Moscow. And other Communist parties either are split and weakened by the Sino-Soviet dispute or have declared their independence from both—a recent major defector being the Communist party of France.

Above all, the fission between Moscow and Peking has produced a major rival for the Kremlin not only in Far Eastern politics but in South Asia, Africa, and virtually every Communist party in the non-communist world. This Chinese rival and its friends have the potential of creating such trouble with the West that the Soviets, unable to prevent hostilities, might be obliged to fight a war they did not provoke, next to allies they distrusted, against a foe they could not defeat.

The Communists are not ten feet tall, and we are not bumbling pygmies by comparison, as a few discouraged and hypertense

Americans would have the rest of us believe. The fact is that the world is changing in the direction we want to see it change. And these changes have been produced not only by the mass miscalculations of the Communist leaders but by the imagination, the energies, and the determination of a couple of dozen free countries, led by a succession of undiscouraged American Presidents.

One symptom of American self-doubt is the view that we are trying to do too much in too many places at too great cost. This is not merely an extension into foreign affairs of the normal tendency of political conservatives to cut down and hold back government programs. Citizens, columnists, and political leaders who on other tests would be classed as liberals also are nagged by the notion that the United States is overextended and overcommitted in world affairs.

The notion is no novelty. It has popped up with tedious frequency in recent decades. In the early days of World War II, there were many who feared that our participation in the war would overextend us. Columnists, then as now, wrote that our commitments were in danger of outdistancing our resources.

No wonder. When Pearl Harbor was attacked on that memorable Sunday, we were so unready for major war that we might almost as well have been starting from scratch. Within months we were committed to raising, training, equipping, and sending overseas a great land army; to designing and building the world's greatest air force, and training the crews to fly it; to constructing the greatest navy ever to sail the seas, capable of operating for extended periods thousand of miles from its bases; to building, from keel on up, the world's largest merchant marine; to feeding the nation even as young men were drained from the farms for fields of battle; to helping supply and feed our British and Soviet allies. In a word, we committed ourselves to fighting two great wars against two powerful enemies on opposite sides of the world at the same time, while providing the critical margin of survival to our wartime partners. By normal standards a rational man could well conclude that we were dangerously, even desperately, overcommitted.

The "impossible took a little longer," as the Seabees said, but we did all of these things—and did them all at the same time—and found that as a by-product we had doubled the productive capacity of the domestic economy of the United States.

Then, not long after the war, the fear returned. Some felt that the United States was overcommitting its resources when it determined to protect Greece and Turkey, mounted the Marshall Plan for the recovery of Europe, and agreed in the North Atlantic Treaty that an attack on any of fourteen allies would be an attack on the United States. The worriers of that time do not doubt now that the Truman Doctrine was a courageous and necessary move, that the Marshall Plan was a wise investment, and NATO an indispensable block to Soviet ambitions in Europe. You can hardly blame them if, in celebrating these American achievements, they forget to mention their earlier worries. The worriers may be cheerfully granted oblivion for their chronic doubts; but they will have to forgive the rest of us if we discount their misgivings now.

In the years since Western Europe held the center of the stage, the people who think that America tries too hard and does too much have had plenty of cause for gloomy headshaking. We fought a war in Korea, defended the Straits of Formosa, helped set up international peace-keeping in the Middle East, sent the Marines to help in Lebanon, airlifted U.N. peace-keepers to the Congo, quarantined Cuba, faced down the Soviet Union over those missiles, helped establish a U.N. peace-keeping operation in Cyprus, and increased our commitment in Vietnam to match the increasing effort of the Communists to destroy the government and take over the people of South Vietnam. At the same time we were mounting a broad attack on poverty in Asia, Africa, and Latin America, which has already graduated several nations from dependence on our support, and shown others some light at the end of the tunnel of economic and social development.

In the course of these exertions we have arrived at something like a tacit understanding that nuclear war had better not be started, and that there is no nourishment in conventional military aggression.

Our current exertions are designed to prove that there is no more mileage in clandestine attack than in overt attack—that in this day and age aggression by any name cannot pay off. Our enemy is not change but violence. We are committed to the proposition that those who wish to change the shape of society must pursue their ambitions by non-violent means. When that lesson is learned at last by the Far Eastern Communists as well as others, this will be a safer and a happier planet.

These exertions have required great commitments in the past, and they still do. But are they any greater today than they were a few years ago? Are they even as great?

In our own armament we reached the point where our power was so enormous that we could safely agree to a treaty banning all but underground nuclear tests. We could afford to cut back on the production of fissionable materials. We could afford to close or reduce 135 major overseas military bases in the four years from 1961 to 1965. And we could afford to lower our over-all defense budget—not much but a little bit absolutely, and a little bit more relatively, because our economy keeps growing at a steady high rate. Only the growth of the Vietnam war turned the budget curve upward again in 1965.

In Europe our presence is still needed; but our commitment is less, in relation to our resources and in relation to those of our allies, than it had to be a dozen years ago. In Vietnam, even the stepped up commitment in manpower and resources during 1965 was but a fraction of our commitment a decade and a half earlier in Korea.

For military aid to allies and friends around the world, our commitments have dropped to about one-third of what they were a decade ago. For economic development under the Foreign Assistance Act our expenditures have dropped from 11.5 per cent of the federal budget in 1949 to about 2 per cent in 1965.

In relation to resources—our physical capacity to fulfill our commitments—we were significantly less extended in 1965 than at almost any time since World War II.

If we are not, then, overextended in a physical sense, have we taken on too big a responsibility for keeping the peace of the world? Are we trying to play the world's gendarme? Are we tending to go it alone, as some anxious voices have asked?

The answer is that we have taken as little direct responsibility for the peace of the world as the safety of that peace would allow us. We have done what we could to induce the world community to assume the responsibility for policing the world. We have tried our best to go it, not alone, but in the largest company we could find to go with us. How we can further widen the community of the concerned is the subject of the rest of this book.

Americans of our generation are privileged to live in a time when the frustrations of American foreign policy are often the agony of success, while the frustrations of Soviet foreign policy are typically the agony of failure.

The Soviets, who do not believe in diversity, failed to take over Western Europe from within. They failed to make a political killing with aid and trade. They failed to destroy the United Nations or blow down anti-communist governments with nuclear terror. They failed to subvert the nationalist revolutions and spark the chain of communist revolts that Lenin dreamed of. They even failed to keep their own bloc glued together.

They failed partly because of Western countermeasures under American leadership and because of U.N. actions we supported. But mostly they failed because peoples and their leaders do not want to be pushed around if there is any alternative.

Crisis Diplomacy

4

Most of the people engaged in the management of American foreign policy are not working most of the time on the headline crises but on other subjects. A round of tariff negotiations, a student exchange program, the use of surplus food for economic growth, the tedious but important process of getting to know hundreds of leading personalities in more than a hundred foreign countries, the analysis of bits and pieces of intelligence from all over the world, the selection and instruction of government delegates to 600 conferences a year—these and many, many other necessary works are also "American foreign policy."

Yet in the upper reaches of our government, and particularly at the level of the President and his nearest echelon of advisers, the management of foreign policy does seem to be the act of throwing ourselves into one crisis after another. The President, the Secretaries of State and Defense, the Director of Central Intelligence, and several dozen other men do spend a very large part of their time working on the crises of the moment.

They spend their time this way because there is no other way for responsible men to take the responsibility for crucial decisions. For the problem of decision making in our complicated world is not how to get the problem simple enough so that we can all understand it; the problem is to get our thinking about the problem as complex as humanly possible, and thus approach (we can never match) the complexity of the real world around us. And only the highest officials are in a position thus to maximize the complexities.

Albert Einstein is supposed to have said that every proposition should be as simple as possible, but not one bit simpler. The decision maker in any large-scale enterprise—and a fortiori the maker of decisions in international affairs—has to immerse himself *personally* in the full complexity of the problem at hand. "Completed staff work" is the last thing he wants, or should want, from his advisers. For if he is to make a responsible decision, he must himself measure the options and filter the imagined consequences of each through his most dependable computer, which is his own brain.

By the same token, "contingency planning" must normally deal with many contingencies that do not, as things work out, come to pass. In the fall of 1962, countless man-hours went into contingency planning for the crises elsewhere that were thought to be the Soviets' possible reaction to a quarantine of Cuba. Yet contingency planning is never wasted, for it develops the analytical skills of the contingency planners and thus puts the government in a more "ready" position.

The most usable end product of planning is not a paper, but a person thoroughly immersed in the subject—a person whose mind is trained to act, having taken everything into account, on the spur of the moment. That is why the ultimate decision maker must himself participate in the planning exercise. A boxer, training for the bout of his life, cannot afford to let his sparring partners do his daily calisthenics for him.

The management of a foreign policy crisis, then, is an exciting, demanding form of organized thinking, in which the maximum degree of complexity must be sifted through the minds of those few men in a position to take the ultimate responsibility for action. And as Josiah Royce said: "Thinking is like loving and dying; each of us must do it for himself."

It is widely and mistakenly believed that the preoccupation of top officials with day-to-day crises makes it inevitable that long range policy is neglected. Long range policy sometimes is neglected, but not, in my own observation, on that account. Indeed it seems to me that forward planning is most neglected on those subjects which have not been raised to high level notice by crisis conditions requiring immediate attention. For it is at moments of crisis that many of our basic long range decisions about foreign policy are made. Most citizens would be surprised to see how often, when the world thinks the men in Washington are working on the next day's tactics, they are instead debating basic issues affecting the long-run growth of law and institutions, the policy dilemmas suddenly illumined in the dead of night by the light of a crisis in Berlin or the Congo or the Dominican Republic or Vietnam.

The management of crisis diplomacy at the Presidential level is thus a rather personal process, a function of style and political instinct as well as rational option weighing. But it seems to me that at least five lessons of general applicability have emerged in recent years from the Cabinet room in the White House, where the makers of policy foregather and our destiny is shaped.

Lesson No. 1: Keep Your Objectives Limited

Somewhere in his writings Emerson advises young people to be very careful in deciding what they most want out of life—for they are likely to get it. A similar, but qualified, principle applies to American foreign policy: Select your objective carefully, for *if it is limited enough* you are quite likely to achieve it. International politics, like our national politics, is the art of the possible, but in international politics the price of overreaching the possible could be nuclear extinction.

In the Cuba missile crises, President Kennedy decided that an adverse shift in the world power balance was in the making, and our basic security interests therefore required the removal of "offensive weapons" from Cuba. That term might be subject to varying interpretations having to do with both weaponry and purpose; but clearly it covered the IRBMs and MRBMs, the IL-28 medium range bombers, and nuclear warheads for these and any other weapons. For this overriding but still limited goal the President was prepared to commit U.S. power and prestige to the hilt.

Critics later said that the objective should have been broader, that the outright elimination of both the Soviet presence and Castro-communism from Cuba should have been the objective in October 1962. But the judgment of the moment, confirmed by the eloquent silence of those critics at the time, was that the missiles and bombers were the only threat so great as to require the immediate counterthreat of force to remove them. The Soviet troops were a dangerous nuisance; we could and did continue our efforts to get them out, and in time they quietly departed. But they did not represent, as the missiles did, a fundamental change in the balance of world power. Castro, too, was a serious problem, but relief from the embarrassment of his presence in the Caribbean was not to be measured in megadeaths throughout the Northern Hemisphere. In the Cuba missile crisis, then, a limited objective was attained brilliantly—because it was specific and attainable.

In the Congo the Administration's objective was a limited one. In 1960 President Eisenhower decided to back a U.N. peace force for the Congo, instead of responding to the new Congolese government's urgent appeal for our direct intervention. Neither then nor since has the U.S. government undertaken to prevent internal trouble in the Congo except to the extent that such trouble invited foreign intervention and therefore threatened (in U.N. Charter language) the Congo's "territorial integrity and political independence."

Even the decision to rescue the hostages at Stanleyville, in 1964, was carefully limited to that one purpose. Some Americans, and some Congolese, thought we should defeat the rebels while we were there. But the restraints which led the Eisenhower and Kennedy Administrations to limit U.S. responsibility for the Congo's internal troubles were equally persuasive to President Johnson; most of the Belgian troops and their U.S. airlift support were withdrawn in less than a week after rescuing 2,500 hostages.

A limited objective has likewise been the key to American policy during the recurring crises in Laos. When confronted by the Communist push in Laos in 1961, the new Administration in Washington was faced with three alternatives: to accept the huge costs and risks of holding Laos with U.S. military force, to allow the country to fall to Communist control, or to seek a settlement based on neutrality. It was decided that a neutral Laos just might have a chance, whereas the effort to affiliate Laos with the free world had helped divide the country by civil war.

As things worked out, the Communists paid little attention to the agreement, and the three-headed International Control Commission continued to be an ineffective peace-keeper. So the civil war resumed, but with a difference: This time the "neutrals" under Souvanna Phouma were convinced that the most dangerous threat to Laotian neutrality came from the Communists and not from the West. Desultory fighting in a semibuffer state was certainly better than an all out effort to make a bastion of so small and rugged a country, populated by so gentle a people, as Laos.

The case of Vietnam is harder to judge because we are still in mid-passage as this is written. The original Geneva agreements were a sound basis for settlement, considering that the French had just lost their war with the North Vietnamese; a line was drawn at the 17th parallel, and elections throughout North and South Vietnam were called for. The agreements were seriously defective in the kind of peace-keeping instrument established to police them. As in Laos, peace-keeping was entrusted to a three-headed commission—latterly we would know it as a "troika"—in which the intransigence of the Polish member and the timidity of the Indian chairman offset the desire of the Canadian member to make it work.

But in Vietnam the objective was larger and fuzzier than has been traditional in our crisis diplomacy. President Eisenhower said our aim was "to assist the government of Vietnam in developing and maintaining a strong, viable state, capable of resisting attempted subversion or aggression through military means." That policy was inherited, and repeated with variations, by Presidents Kennedy and Johnson; and it had to be backed by increasing inputs of U.S. military power as the North Vietnamese, finding it impossible to subvert South Vietnam by organizing an "indigenous" rebellion, started manning and equipping the Viet Cong revolt more and more professionally, and more and more obviously.

The generalized aim of our policy still served as justification for our action, but even our closest allies thought we had gotten in too deep. In early 1965, President Johnson offered "unconditional discussions" about peace; the Communists did not yet think they were stalemated by our power, and did not immediately respond. But once a military stalemate could be achieved, it was already clear that our vital interests in forcing Hanoi to "leave its neighbor alone" would have to be defined in more explicit, which is to say more limited, terms. In the oft repeated Eisenhower form, the purpose of our policy was too open-ended for comfort.

What the United States did in 1965 about the breakdown of law and order in the Dominican Republic illustrated again the importance of limiting our efforts to attainable aims. The comparatively large size of the military force put ashore at Santo Domingo obscured the fact that its orders were to hold a single corridor as a safe haven—a base from which foreigners could be evacuated, and an island of relative safety to which the foreigners who remained, and Dominicans uninvolved in the fighting, could repair for protection. As things worked out, this corridor was endorsed by the Organization of American States and our troops eventually merged into an Inter-American Peace Force, still holding the same enclave.

The geography of the corridor was well selected: it became in time a physical barrier to further fighting between the two main armed factions, and thus enabled the OAS to tackle the longer and more difficult part of the peace-keeping task, the construction of a government with enough Dominican talent and consent to start the little nation toward public order and economic development. If President Johnson had selected a broader initial objective for our forces, such as the occupation of the entire country or even the whole city of Santo Domingo, he would have enormously complicated the task of passing the peace-keeping task to the OAS, and lengthened the time before he could start pulling out our own forces. If a nation has the strength, which we do, it is always relatively easy to get into a messy situation overseas; the difficult thing is to get out. And the key to getting out is careful limitation of the stated reasons for going in.

In crises that involve other nations in the free world and not directly the Soviet Union or Communist China, the U.S. objective can be more limited than in Southeast Asia or Cuba or even the Congo. When, for example, the French and Tunisians fell to fighting over the base at Bizerte, our considerable diplomatic efforts were bent toward the limited aim of keeping the peace. The same has been true at several stages of the Kashmir dispute which risks setting off a renewal of communal killing that no peace-keeping force on earth could contain. We cannot escape either our own power or our obligations under the U.N. Charter; both propel us into the middle of any dispute that threatens to disturb the peace. But in such disputes, our primary interest is in getting the disputants to talk rather than fight; any outcome agreed between the parties most concerned is likely to be all right with us.

Similarly, during recurrent recent "flaps" on Israel's borders and among the Arab countries, our concern is essentially with procedure rather than with trying to play God on the substance of local disputes. That Israel is here to stay is a basic tenet of American foreign policy; but when it comes to frontier flare-ups, our effort generally is focused on setting up a procedure for defusing border incidents, case by case. This interest in procedure has caused the United States to initiate, or support, a whole network of U.N. tripwires and conciliation devices: the Mixed Armistice Commissions, the Truce Supervisory Organization, the U.N. Emergency Force in the Gaza Strip and along the Israeli-Egyptian frontier, a U.N. presence in Jordan, and, for a limited time, an abortive agreement for a U.N.-inspected evacuation of foreign troops and military aid from Yemen.

In all these examples our objectives are limited, not by some absolute yardstick, but by a relative standard which matches them with our vital interests. Since our "must" list cannot include everything we would like to see happen in a turbulent world, the first task of crisis diplomacy is to decide what immediate aims are really worth the impressive resources we can deploy to achieve them.

Lesson No. 2: Decide How Far You Would Go

Having limited his aims to match the vital interests of the United States, an American President facing a foreign policy crisis must make another decision: how far down the road to the use of force he will, realistically, be willing to travel if things go from bad to worse. This is partly a judgment about his allies: Who will be with him in the first instance, and in the last? But in the ultimate clutch would he—honestly, now—order U.S. armed forces into action to support the policy, and if so, on what scale?

It is these questions that had to be faced in 1954, when the commitment was made to defend South Vietnam. Only with the passage of time and the escalation of the Communist effort to take over South Vietnam by force did the full enormity of that blank check appear, as it was cashed in larger and larger installments. Once a commitment is made, the President who makes it and his successors can never quite roll back history and unmake it. How the United States honors the commitment, once it is seriously challenged, affects every part of a global network of U.S. commitments; what we do in Vietnam is watched with prayer and passion in Berlin as well as Bangkok. It is watched, too, with cold calculation in the capitals of those nations that have declared themselves our adversaries.

Some version of the "decide how far you would go" question must also be asked by decision makers elsewhere, including those in the Kremlin. But in a democratic society so powerful that it must lead, not follow, the early facing of these questions is of the essence. For in matters of life and death, a democracy cannot bluff. It has to mean business.

A democratic government can, for a little while at least, cloak its tactics in official secrecy. But it does well to assume that its ultimate intentions are bound to show. Many people are looking on; some are asking questions; there is too much tradition and habit and impulse toward openness for a democracy to keep a very big secret very long. And while this adds to the frustrations of doing business in world affairs, it is, in the end, not a price but a blessing of diversity.

In the crisis over Soviet missile bases in Cuba, it was plain as day that the United States would, if need be, eliminate them by force—and alone if necessary. It was this very clarity of resolve which made our quarantine action, that relatively restrained first response, so extraordinarily effective. The Soviets had to work into their calculations not just the effect of a naval quarantine, but their own willingness to escalate to hostilities that might lead to nuclear war as the price of keeping their missiles on an island off Florida. Looked at this way, it simply did not seem worth while, and they took the missiles and bombers out.

In the Congo, it was clear from the outset that if the Soviets threatened to introduce a military presence in Central Africa, we would have to reply in kind. It was one of the last things we wanted to have happen—which mainly accounts for our consistent support of the alternative afforded by the United Nations.

Perhaps it will illuminate the central importance of deciding about the ultimate use of force if we note some cases closer to the other end of the crisis spectrum.

When the Indonesians and the Dutch squared off on West New Guinea in 1962, we looked around to see who was interested in the matter in a practical way. The Dutch were interested, not in retaining control of West New Guinea, which they had tried very hard to give to the United Nations, but in giving it up with dignity under arrangements that guaranteed to the Papuans the right of deciding their own destiny. The Australians were watching matters closely, and with deep concern. The Indonesians were anxious to take over the territory, and seemed for a time to be willing to do so by force. The Soviets clearly had an interest, as the principal supplier of military equipment to Indonesia. And we were interested, because a solution by force would have been in the interests of nobody, except perhaps the Soviets.

The problem, therefore, was to get a peaceful settlement agreed to by both Dutch and Indonesians. The Secretary-General of the United Nations chose an American diplomat, Ellsworth Bunker, to bring the parties together, and it was this mediator who finally proposed the arrangement that neither government could suggest but both could accept. The bedrock fact was this: There was no disposition, in the Netherlands or among her closest allies, to insist upon a different result if that meant the use of military force.

At the softest end of the spectrum, there is the case of Goa. The future of this Portuguese enclave in India should have been negotiated, as had already been done with the similar French and British enclaves. The Goans themselves might well have been asked what they thought about their future, but neither side was prepared to ask them. Our government and other governments worked hard behind the scenes to get talks started and to prevent the use of force in Goa. But the Indians did not want to wait any longer, and the Portuguese did not want to talk.

When the crunch came, the United States like other governments had to face up honestly to whether it was prepared to defend Goa from the Indians, and had to concede that this would not be a prudent and sensible use of American armed forces. As an exercise in random opinion sampling, I have asked hundreds of Americans since then whether they would have wanted to put the Marines into Goa, or even go there themselves to fight. I have yet to find a volunteer.

Since nobody was prepared to stop the Indians by force, there was no possibility of the United Nations "doing something" about Goa. We and others publicly complained, with irrefutable logic, that India's use of military force to accomplish the takeover was in flat violation of her commitments under the Charter. But we and other military powers are the Charter's teeth; in cases where we are not prepared to bite, the United Nations' only recourse is moral suasion—and the Indians knew it.

Lesson No. 3: Creep Up Carefully on the Use of Force

The "next step" in a foreign crisis depends, then, on what limits are set to the objectives sought, and how far we are willing to go to achieve them. But even if the responsible executive decides he is willing to risk nuclear war for an objective of vital concern, it behooves him to select first the gentlest form of force that has a good chance of being effective.

The purpose of using force is not to kill people we fear, nor is it to provide a release for the frustrations of the user. It is to accomplish the limited objective sought in the particular case, with the least risk of escalation to more damaging forms of force.

Thus in the Cuban crisis, the advantage of a naval quarantine over an air strike was that it put the option of starting violent action up to the Soviets, and gave them forty-eight hours (the time it would take the nearest Soviet freighter to reach the quarantine line) to think it over. Now, with hindsight wisdom, we know that decision was right. Latent power worked so well that power in being was never engaged at all.

Responsible political leaders will always start the use of force at the cautious end of the spectrum of possibilities, for force is a one-way moving staircase; it is easy to escalate, very hard to de-escalate. Much theoretical argument and many books on ther-monuclear war have partly obscured the very wide range of lesser ways to apply force. Yet it is precisely in the controlled, political use of force that we have useful current experience.

We know that, once the decision is made to go much further if necessary, many moves short of war are both possible and effective. We can move military equipment around to dramatize our resolve—as in positioning tanks in Friedrichstrasse in Berlin or moving the Seventh Fleet into the Formosa Strait. We can shift ground forces into positions of readiness for quick action—as in the placement of American troops on the Thai border during the Laos crisis of 1962. We can inject a military force into a trouble spot to keep the lid from blowing off, and then encourage the United Nations or a regional organization to take a hand—as President Eisenhower did in 1958 by landing Marines in Lebanon, and President Johnson did in 1965 by sending troops to the Dominican Republic. We can help finance and provide logistic support to a U.N. peace force, as we have done for nine years in the Middle East and did for four years in the Congo. And even where acts of war seem to be required, they can be used to make a political point. The bombing of North Vietnam announced—some weeks before Secretary Rusk formulated it as public doctrine—the end of the era in which secret aggressors could count on sanctuary for the military bases from which the aggression was prepared and launched.

In the hands of rational men, the escalator to nuclear war comes equipped with many steps and plenty of occasions for much talk along the way.

The use of force in a dangerous world therefore demands adherence to a doctrine of restraint: the cool, calm, and collected manipulation of power for collective security, and the sophisticated mixture of diplomacy, not instead of the force but right along with it. Until the ultimate thermonuclear button is pressed and mutual destruction evolves from mutual desperation, force is just another manner of speaking—with a rather expensive vocabulary. But if force is to be a persuasive form of discourse, its modulations must carry not only the latent threat of more force but equally the assurance that is under the personal control of responsible men.

Lesson No. 4: Widen the Community of the Concerned

The unilateral use of power is becoming as old-fashioned as horse cavalry. Even when the decision to employ power is essentially our own, we find it highly desirable to widen the community of the concerned—to obtain sanction for the necessary "next step" from the broadest practicable segment of the international community.

It was President Truman who made the first decision to stand against aggression in Korea, and it was ultimately American power that enabled the South Koreans to throw it back. But on the day of the President's decision the U.S. government went into the U.N. Security Council and transformed our own resolve into a system of collective security. Acting as executive agent of the United Nations, we later welcomed the participation of fourteen other nations in the defense of Korea.

Each time action has been required to keep the lid on in the Middle East, we have helped strengthen the U.N. presence there, rather than building up our own. Even in 1958, when action seemed to be needed so quickly in Lebanon that the President sent the Army and Marines sloshing ashore, we offered from the outset to get out as quickly as a U.N. force could be mustered to take our place, and made good on this promise in less than three months. The Congo is another clear case where, presented with the option of going in ourselves or helping organize a more complicated, more widely based U.N. force, the U.S. government of the day had no hesitation in choosing the wider over the narrower base of action.

The 1965 intervention in the Dominican Republic, which was widely viewed at the time as an example of unilateral action by the United States, was quickly internationalized. At the time that process seemed agonizingly slow, but it was only weeks before we were able to associate our peace-keeping forces with the troops of five other countries, including a sizable contingent from Brazil. And even before that, the OAS had taken jurisdiction of the problem, sent a peace mission to the island, and voted an international mandate for the foreign troops on Dominican soil.

In the Cuba missile crisis, the decision to apply American power was enveloped from the very outset in a plan for widening the communities of the concerned. In the hours before President Kennedy unveiled the Cuba scenario in his television speech of October 22, dozens of allies were made privy to our plan of action. While the President was speaking, a formal request for an emergency meeting of the Security Council was delivered to its president. The next morning Secretary Rusk presented to the Organization of American States in emergency meeting a proposal for collective action; and that afternoon the Rio Pact nations decided on a quarantine of Cuba and continued aerial surveillance as minimum first steps. The same afternoon, Ambassador Adlai Stevenson opened in the Security Council the case for the United States.

And not until that evening, October 23, did President Kennedy, acting under the Rio Pact, proclaim the quarantine.

In the days that followed, the United Nations went to work in three different ways. It served as the forum in which we could demonstrate the credibility of our evidence about the Soviet missile sites, and explain to the world why we and our Latin American allies had to act on this evidence. Then the United Nations, through the Secretary-General, served as a middleman in crucial parts of the dialogue between President Kennedy and Chairman Khrushchev which led to a peaceful solution. It was an appeal from U Thant that Khrushchev was answering when he said his ships would not challenge the quarantine line. Finally, the United Nations was ready, at our suggestion, to provide inspectors to examine missile sites in Cuba, to make sure the missiles were gone.

Castro, as we know, would not allow U.N. inspectors into his island. But while we would have preferred to have him accept on-site inspection, his refusal to cooperate with the United Nations had useful side effects. For Castro thus branded himself an outlaw, and convinced practically all the vocal bystanders that this was not a case of little Cuba versus the big United States; this was intransigent Cuba thumbing its nose at the world community.

The object of our policy was to get rid of those missiles and bombers, peacefully if possible. There is no doubt that diplomatic operations in the Organization of American States and the United Nations had much to do with the fact that most of the world came to agree with this aim, and thus helped to achieve it.

In recent times, only in Vietnam has an international way of attacking a major problem eluded us. We have consulted frequently with Atlantic allies, kept in touch with Far Eastern allies, and kept up a running dialogue with the Secretary-General of the United Nations. But the Hanoi government and its friends in Peking had accepted no general obligations and were not a part of any international peace system whose machinery could be invoked.

And the *ad hoc* arrangements designed at Geneva to substitute for the United Nations turned sour almost from the moment they were signed. As this is written, the attempts to inject our allies, or the United Nations, or groups of non-aligned nations, or even the Soviets, as mediators in the dispute have served only to demonstrate how reluctant are the Far Eastern Communists to be caught anywhere near a conference room.

In spite of this experience, it is fair to say that in every crisis it is U.S. policy to merge our efforts with the efforts of others as much as we can—which is a function of the willingness of others as well as ourselves. We do not think merging our efforts with others subtracts anything from our "national sovereignty," nor does it inhibit something called our "freedom of action." Notions like these are a hangover from the now obsolete assumption that, acting alone, we are sovereign and free. In these days of interdependence, a stronger case can be made for the contrary proposition: that in each crisis we are born naked, and we achieve freedom of action by using our power in concert with whatever group of nations is most relevant to the task at hand. That this is true of little countries hardly needs to be argued; it is, indeed, why most small nations are so partial to the United Nations. That it is becoming true of all countries, even the most powerful, is one of the lessons of each foreign policy crisis in our time.

The matrix of alliances and international organizations, more even than the power of individual nations, is the hallmark of modern international relations. We will return to these parcels of the general peace in the chapters that follow.

Lesson No. 5: The Law You Make May Be Your Own

In the ebb and flow of crisis diplomacy, those who watch the "Flash" and "Critic" cables and write the contingency papers are very much involved with international law, and with its unanswered questions. Laymen as well as lawyers can readily perceive how principles that are valid in one area may be silly in another, how improvised instruments tend to harden into permanent institutions, how scientific invention and technological innovation outrace man's thinking about law, how old doctrine grows obsolete and gets altered in practice. So the final "lesson from crises I have known" is this: Watch carefully the precedents you set. You will have to live with the institutions you create. The law you make may be your own.

Consider, as a choice and current example, the mutations in the doctrine of sovereignty over air space. The law used to be simple: You cannot fly through my air space unless I say you can. But two large holes have now been knocked through this law, one by the necessities of collective security and the other by the imperative of space technology.

The security hole is best illustrated by the outcome of the Cuba missile crisis. We said we wanted to be sure the missiles left Cuba and did not secretly return. For this purpose, we judged from experience, Castro's Cuba would have to be carefully watched. We were quite prepared to have U.N. inspectors do the watching, provided they did it efficiently and let us know what they saw. Castro did not agree to any of the several formulas for U.N. surveillance proposed to him by Secretary-General U Thant. This in turn justified us in continuing our own aerial observation (as authorized by the regional security organization, the OAS) without having to keep secret the fact that we were doing it.

So the new principle, if there is one, would read something like this: You must stay out of my air space unless you can demonstrate to the satisfaction of the relevant international organizations that I am inclined to do dangerous things and that I will not accept international inspection to ensure that I don't do them.

The other big factor that makes the old doctrine of air space obsolescent is this: What if I fly over your nation in *outer* space, above the "air"? Cameras can now see more from a hundred miles than they used to be able to see from five. Both Soviet and U.S.

space capsules are orbiting frequently in outer space, which has been declared freer than air by unanimous resolution of the U.N. General Assembly. So the doctrine that nations control the space above their sovereign soil runs out of gas somewhere in the upper stratosphere. Just how far up that point is, neither the scientists nor the lawyers, let alone the General Assembly, have yet been prepared to say. Maybe the march of technology has made this one of the questions in international law that no longer matter much anyway.

When we put all these lessons together, perhaps we have nothing more than another, more up-to-date, way of thinking about political leadership in its most complex form. I have said that the decision maker in time of crisis (which now means all the time) must keep his objective in line with his nation's vital interests, must decide how far he would ultimately go, must use force gently while widening the community of the concerned, and must set only those precedents he would be willing to live with later.

If the known factors and the rational considerations indicate a clear preference for one policy alternative over any other, then decision making is easy, and responsible criticism correspondingly more difficult. That is why such decisions seldom reach the Secretary of State or the President. It is when a rational weighing of measurable factors still leaves two or more reasonable options that the man who makes the ultimate decision must somehow stuff the whole problem into his own head, and add those priceless ingredients: personal judgment, sense of direction, feel for the total political environment in which the decision is made.

The fact that the most important decisions are often close decisions, that the personal judgment of political leaders is so deeply involved, makes them peculiarly easy to criticize. But the responsible critic of foreign policy decisions must also wrap his mind around the full complexity of the problem. He too must think in terms of limited objectives; he too must decide when and where he would use force, how he would deal with allies and neutrals, what laws and institutions he is prepared to make—or break. If the critic is not willing to propose an alternative policy that meets these tests of relevance, then he is not criticizing American foreign policy but merely scratching an itch of his own.

At the moment of action the man who has to take the personal responsibility for the final decision, and face the political cross fire it may produce, is alone with his own understanding, his own moral gyroscope, and his own fund of courage. It takes no courage to bluster; it takes some to stand up to a mortal threat that plainly has to be faced. But what takes the most gumption is to persevere in a decision that takes months or years to prove itself.

There were moments during the chronic Congo crisis when the brickbats were very thick in Washington; but President Kennedy stuck to his position, simply because the alternative of great-power confrontation in the middle of Africa seemed even more unattractive than the swelling noise level on his Congo policy. More recently, President Johnson's actions in Vietnam have been the target of teach-ins and Senatorial tirades. But he stuck to his mix of force and diplomacy because none of the alternatives, from pulling out to bombing Peking, seemed better calculated to serve our nation's interests as he saw them.

The capacity to keep on working with brickbats whizzing past the ears is, of course, the first qualification for public leadership in an open society. But the saving grace in the management of foreign policy is this: Dyspeptic criticism of actions that turn out to be successful has a very short half-life.

obscure program

Peace Comes in Parcels

5

We live in a world where the imperatives of modern technology increasingly require us to merge national interests in international jurisdictions for such purposes as aerial navigation and weather forecasting and the use of radio frequencies and a hundred other examples.

Yet for better or for worse, we also live in a world of fervent nationalism and well-marked national frontiers.

Common interest and common sense have drawn the nations in recent years into an impressive start toward building an international community of common institutions working away at scores of practical and urgent tasks—and some exhilarating tasks, too, such as stamping out malaria, and providing hot lunches for undernourished school children.

Yet nationalism has, if anything, been a rising fever in recent years, and not only in the newest of the nations.

Three-quarters of our planet is covered by water free from claims by nations. In outer space where the satellites fly there is no place at all for national sovereignty. Celestial bodies have been declared off limits to nationalism, by unanimous resolution of the General Assembly of the United Nations.

Yet that same Assembly has been reluctant to tell the nations of which it is composed that they must pay what the Assembly says they owe the United Nations for helping keep the peace. And no U.N. member questions the right of a few major nations to a Security Council veto—that sturdy symbol of the principle of national sovereignty in the very heart of international organization.

Nations are here to stay; and it takes two of them to tango, and quite a few more to execute the modern choreography of multilateral cooperation in the era of complex technology and accelerating change. To cooperate means that two or more nations must be equally prepared to forego claims of exclusive national sovereignty over some field of activity, or to admit that the march of science has already removed their claim from the realm of reason.

Nothing illustrates this better than the failure of the so-called Baruch Plan in the very first years of the United Nations. Under this proposal—which seems even more sensational in retrospect than it seemed at the time—the United States was prepared to transfer to an international agency exclusive sovereignty over those processes in nuclear science which could lead to the production of nuclear weapons. For two long years of windy debate, the Soviet Union did not budge from its initial position that this proposal was an unwarranted, impossible, and insidious effort to infringe the sovereignty of the Soviet Union.

To this day, the Soviet Union has been unable to bring itself to admit inspection teams to verify that underground disturbances are earthquakes and not tests of nuclear bombs. Only a few visits a year would be needed for this purpose. They could be brief. The inspected areas would be very limited. The inspection teams would be under Russian surveillance on Soviet soil. They could even be blindfolded on the way in and out. And still the answer is "no."

This is why the first test ban agreement did not cover underground tests. Such is the grip of the concept of sovereignty and the related system of secrecy on that nation with which we must primarily seek agreements bearing on world peace and world order. And such is the reluctance, shared in some degree by all nations, which stands in the way of establishing a world organization to guarantee the peace.

No great Peace Conference or Constitutional Convention, clearly, will weld the world into amiable solidarity. International bargaining about arms control and borders and trade and human rights and self-determination will be an enduring feature of the political landscape.

We can thank our stars—and our diplomats—that the United Nations has been able to damp down a series of dangerous conflicts which could have raged out of control. But, somehow, we *are* better at discouraging violence than at devising settlements that endure. Korea, Kashmir, the Congo, Cyprus, and the Arab-Israeli conflict bear witness. Stopping the bloodshed has not settled the basic problems that cause the bloodshed and that could bring on a renewal of mutual murder.

The same is true of the relations between the great powers. The nations that know the most about nuclear armament have looked deeply into the dangers, and have signed nuclear test bans, and started talking about reducing the amount of fissionable materials in the world. But the problems which created the nuclear arms race—the thwarted Communist ambitions of which a divided Berlin, a divided Korea, and a divided Vietnam are the continuing symbols—are not settled, merely stalemated.

Given the persistence of dangerous rivalries over real issues, how are we going to build a system of order in which ideas can clash and talented men can compete without killing each other? The American answer comes naturally out of the American experience. If we are not prepared to have any one group or party grasp a monopoly of relevant power in our own society, it follows that world peace is far too large a responsibility to entrust to any one "system" or institution. The whole task of keeping the peace of the world, which includes making or permitting the necessary changes without violence, is, we think, beyond the capacity of any group of human beings who might conceivably be given the job, or arrogate it to themselves.

It is therefore advisable for Americans, who must decide how to use their power in an explosive world, to think of peace not as a goal but as a process. No one institution will make all the decisions and no one agreement will record them. All nations will have some voice, and each of the various and differentiated organizations they establish together will "make" a part of the "peace." The idea that any one nation, however big or rich or talented, should run the whole planet is recognized as a monstrous presumption. The idea that some single central authority could devise and administer and secure world peace is equally illusory.

As we "search" for "peace," therefore, we had best think of it as a growing complex of procedures for cooperating with others to pursue interests that are recognized as common, a complicated web of agreements, some written but most unwritten, to take "next steps" together. These "next steps" are many, urgent, and obvious: a map of a disputed frontier, a ban on nuclear testing, a standby peace force, a regional security system, a common market, a weather forecasting system, a smallpox eradication program, a program to make sure the world's children get enough to eat, a literacy campaign, a standing army of technical experts for economic and social development.

To think of peace in parcels may seem to increase the complexity of the undertaking. But, more important, it decreases the complexity of the parts. For we can then think more clearly about how to break the job into more manageable assignments—limited tasks that may be do-able by limited, fallible mortals working through the imperfect institutions that we humans are accustomed to build and operate.

And we can even begin to use a somewhat different vocabulary from the abstractions called "peace" and "order" and "law." We can stress the verbs rather than the nouns, and talk more about *containing* conflict, *managing* crises, *promoting* necessary change, and *administering* the institutions of peace.

In this kind of world, the process of creating a tolerable order requires us to work at several levels, through a wide variety of institutions, and with a mix of techniques at one and the same time. It is not a very precise process, nor is it amenable to precise planning.

Nonetheless we can plot out the major avenues toward a workable system of international order; and we can identify a rough hierarchy of levels at which order can be organized and pragmatic "next steps" taken.

The first level—and it is all too easy to overlook—is the nation-to-nation relationships. Treaties of peace and friendship, agreements for the joint use and development of resources, settlement of disputes through negotiation, mediation, arbitration, or recourse to an international court, joint instruments, joint ventures, joint control boards, joint claims settlement commissions—all these add up to a large, if dwindling, proportion of international relations.

Most nations do in fact maintain tolerably orderly relations with their neighbors. (Our relations with Canada are so good that Canadian pundits and politicians sometimes complain the United States does not pay enough attention to them.) International disputes claim our attention because they are exceptional; but international cooperation is the rule in world affairs. This is not because it is natural for nations to be nice to each other, but because they find it advantageous to swallow part of their pride and bury part of their sovereignty in working with each other for mutual safety and progress.

A rapidly growing part of international relations now takes the form of organizations and conferences in which not two but many nations assume obligations toward each other and establish international executives to police and administer them. Not long ago an American ambassador in a medium-sized country told me that 75 per cent of the work load on his desk consisted of multilateral matters, that is, issues arising in an international organization or conference requiring the ambassador to discuss them bilaterally with the country to which he was accredited.

It is obviously true that multilateral bodies are the usual forum for such issues as disarmament, alliance policy, and the 100 standard items on the agenda of the U.N. General Assembly. But the same thing has come to be true of most trade and economic matters. Our trade negotiations are mostly with the GATT (General Agreement on Tariffs and Trade); the chief overseas concern of U.S. farmers is with international commodity agreements; trade with Communist countries is regulated by an international committee. It is increasingly noticeable, in every specialized field from analphabetism to zinc, that we consult with just about everybody on just about everything.

For this purpose the United States belongs to 53 international organizations, and attended 633 international conferences in the twelve months ending June 30, 1965. During the nineteenth century the United States participated in an average of one conference a year; now we go to more than 600 a year. In the twenty-four months ending in mid-1965, we went to more conferences than the U.S. government attended in its entire national history from 1789 to 1943, the year the U.N. system began at a food conference at Hot Springs, Virginia. (These figures count only government-to-government arrangements. There are 1,469 private international organizations that we know of, and they spawn perhaps 3,000 nongovernmental international conferences a year.)

Most of these conferences do not make general news; only 110 of the 540 conferences we attended in 1964 were mentioned at all in the newspaper with the largest coverage, *The New York Times*. Thus, most people do not realize what an enormous amount of business is transacted in specialized meetings on hundreds of subjects.

It used to be said that American foreign policy had no domestic "constituency." The Department of Agriculture has the farmers, so the argument ran; Commerce has the business community; Labor has the trade unions. But the State Department has only the foreigners—and they do not vote. It is true that foreigners do not vote in American elections (though we sometimes find ourselves watching *their* elections rather carefully). But the Americans who want to cooperate with foreigners do vote. And on nearly every subject under the sun there are vocal and active groups which insist on cooperating across national frontiers. The State Department used to worry about the apathy and disinterest of Americans concerning international affairs. Now it worries about all the pressure groups which will complain loudly on Capitol Hill if more and more cooperation is not facilitated by the bureaucrats in Washington.

Today, a U.S. foreign policy based on cooperation has an American constituency as wide as the continent and as deep as man's instinct for survival and growth. It may be that the State Department's newly awakened "constituents" do not understand everything their government is doing abroad. It may be that they want their tax money spent for their own kind of cooperation but want to economize on those kinds of cooperation from which they see on direct pay-off. It may be that the people interested in coffee prices or tuna fishing rights or malaria eradication or refugee relief or investment guarantees sometimes fail to see the connection between their specialized interest and the healthy growth of a North Atlantic alliance or a U.N. peace-keeping system. But every American has some stake in some form of functional international cooperation—and most Americans now know it.

Beyond bilateral deals and specialized multilateral dealings, there is the regional level of cooperation. Neighbors should first settle their own disputes; that is the conventional wisdom. It has a long and distinguished lineage.

The story of man can be told in terms of his increasing capacity, spurred by new technologies, to widen the community of which he can feel a part. It was no more than 10,000 years ago, a mere blinking of history's eye, that man discovered how to grow his own food and thus make "settlements" possible. We can see that now as an epic technological breakthrough, and its social fallout was the beginning of communities in which human beings learned to live together by living together.

When future historians look back on the decades immediately following World War II, they will surely write it down that our present times were notable for another breakthrough—a system of international communication and a development of explosive power which made it both possible and necessary to build international communities of continental scale. It may be that the fashioning of these communities, overlapping and interacting, will be seen as the most dynamic political force of the twentieth century. In the age of jets, the impassable deserts and impenetrable jungles of Asia and Africa suddenly lost much of their relevance; great oceans that once served as hostile barriers between nations became friendly lakes for communities around their shores. And the writers of world history will be bound to note that the nation with the closest links to most of the new commonwealths was the United States of America.

There is no major area in the whole free world where impulses toward unification, integration, or partnership among neighbors are not yeastily at work. Only among the various kinds of Communists is the trend in the opposite direction.

The most spectacular of these regional developments is of course in Western Europe, where nations that have been at war with each other off and on for most of the modern era are now groping in the general direction of unity. Europe's economic recovery during the Marshall Plan, and a sense of imminent danger from a powerful Soviet Union, brought into being a powerful North Atlantic alliance and, in the economic sphere, a solid institutional achievement: a Common Market covering the world's second greatest industrial complex to serve more than 300 million prospering consumers. Other efforts—a common defense community, the embryo forms of political unity—have been caught in ditches or held up by roadblocks. Nationalism is not as dead as some of the early "Europeans" thought. But real integration of nations is still more likely, sooner, in Western Europe than anywhere else in the world. Our friend the future historian will see the present check to European integration (so most Americans and their government yet believe) as a big bump in a road that has some hazardous stretches but leads in a clearly marked direction.

Part of the early thinking about European integration was that unity would enable continental Europe to join with Britain, Canada, and the United States in something called the Atlantic Community. The obstacles to continental unity have focused more attention on what can be done at the Atlantic level, where a military alliance and a system of political consultation provide the structure within which the United States can exercise its leadership and use its resources to shore up the defense of Europe without downgrading the dignity of the defenders. The alternative, that we lose interest in Europe, is not morally or militarily in the cards.

In the Western Hemisphere a long and somewhat shoddy history of intervention and exploitation has led at last to inter-American institutions where most Latin Americans do not have to feel like second-class citizens of the larger commonwealth. The peoples and even the governments of at least half the Latin countries are beginning to act as if they had something in common besides a common heritage, and poverty. The Organization of American States, the Rio Treaty, the Alliance for Progress, the widespread resentment of Soviet intervention in Cuba—all are symbols of a new sense of community, still inadequately expressed in workable institutions. There are the beginnings of two customs unions, one in Central America and one, the Latin American Free Trade Association, consisting of the principal South American countries and Mexico. And by a recent agreement, the nations of the hemisphere are now reviewing each other's economic programs along lines consciously patterned after European cooperation during the Marshall Plan.

The OAS has helped settle thirty disputes since World War II, but there is a far distance still to go. The collapse of all authority in the Dominican Republic during 1965, and the resulting U.S. intervention there, again illuminated the fundamental dilemma of our own foreign policy: Whenever international machinery cannot be mobilized to keep the peace, sudden violence draws in the world's residual peace-keeper, who is the President of the United States. The "plus" in the peace-keeping equation was there, however, even in the Dominican case: the continuous willingness of the United States to internationalize the basis for action. Thus out of our unilateral action came the hemisphere's first regional peace-keeping force. The Latin Americans can take out insurance against any more U.S. interventions by constructing instead the kind of regional peace-keeping machinery which can, in a pinch, preserve the option of freedom for their neighbors and help them build governments that govern.

In Africa, the regional Organization for African Unity is still not an organization but a periodic conference for issuing manifestoes and setting up committees, without much executive machinery to carry out agreed purposes. But while still in its swaddling clothes it faced up to nasty conflicts between Morocco and Algeria and between Ethiopia and Somalia. The resulting arrangements are in the tradition of Kashmir and the Middle East —cease-fires, not political settlements. The underlying problems have not been made to disappear. But quiet exhortation in the name of African solidarity helped put the lid back on two prospective wars, and that is no small service to the region and the world. The Congo, on the other hand, proved too large and prickly for the OAU to swallow, for reasons which the United States, the Soviet Union, and the United Nations can all understand, since they, too, have all tried their hand in Congolese politics.

In other areas of the world the divisions are more obvious than the efforts at integration of any kind. But in North Africa there is talk of a Maghreb confederation. In the Arab world, cultural unity might lead to political and economic cooperation if the Arabs can decide on something more constructive to cooperate about than the unattainable ambition to push the Israelis into the Mediterranean Sea. In Southeast Asia, President Johnson was plucking a resonant string when he called for regional cooperation in developing the Lower Mekong Basin, and promised to invest in an Asian Development Bank. There is even scholarly talk, still empty of discernible content, about a Pacific community of nations that rim the world's greatest ocean, and the bits and pieces of dry land that dot its surface.

Several years ago Sir Oliver Franks (now Lord Franks) drew a careful bead on this postwar trend and described regionalism as "a halfway house at a time when single nations are no longer viable and the world is not ready to become one." It would be hard to say it better.

The growth of regional communities is quite in line with the obligations of every member of the United Nations. The U.N. Charter explicitly recognizes them. In Article 33, "resort to regional agencies or arrangements" is grouped with other peaceful means which parties to a dispute should use "first of all." And in Article 52, U.N. members are enjoined to settle their disputes if they can through regional procedures "before" resorting to the U.N. Security Council. Some of the United Nations' own economic work is organized in regional commissions, which spawn other regional groupings like the Mekong River project in Southeast Asia.

The idea is that regional organizations can relieve the United Nations of burdens which otherwise might sink the universal boat we are in together. Participation in these overlapping communities of the free is at the doctrinal heart of U.S. foreign policy. This is why we Americans carry around, without embarrassment, a whole pocketful of memberships and associate memberships in interlocking and mutually reinforcing regional bodies. Just now we belong to twenty-two of them—ten in our own hemisphere, twelve in Europe and Asia and Africa. If you can name all of them, you are a very unusual reader.

The notion that neighbors should take the first crack at peace-making in their own backyards thus has some standing and some validity. It especially appeals to the generation of Americans that was brought up on "geopolitics," an interpretation of world affairs which leaned heavily on distance and propinquity to explain the behavior of nations.

But cousins and in-laws are not necessarily the best peace-makers in a family dispute; in the same way and for similar reasons, near neighbors are often undependable allies of peaceful process. It is, in fact, noticeable that nations are usually quicker to suggest ready solutions for conflicts in other regions than in their own. Sometimes I think the first principle of international relations is that courage to engage in peacemaking is directly proportional to distance from the dispute.

Thus, for example, India was prepared to send a 5,000-man brigade to join the U.N. peace-keeping force 4,250 miles away in the Congo; yet it has felt diffident about exercising its muscles in nearby Laos, where India is supposed to act as chairman (and therefore executive agent) of the International Control Commission. The United Kingdom sometimes seems more certain of its defense commitments in Malaysia than in Middle Europe. And even in our own foreign policy, we are quicker to commit substantial force in Vietnam than in Cuba.

That is why we have recourse so often—on a dozen major occasions, and on dozens of lesser issues, during its first twenty years—to the peace-keeping machinery of the United Nations. One of the constants in U.S. foreign policy has been the effort to endow the United Nations with a growing capacity to act, and not merely to talk, for peace. The extent of this capacity, and the limitations on its use, are the subject of our next chapter.

The men and women who wrote the Charter knew well that the

United Nations could be only the central part of a pluralistic peace system. They assumed it would be more relevant than it has been so far to the world's major security problems: the threat of nuclear war, and cases of major aggression. But the machinery they projected in the Charter was fashioned on the clear assumption that the United Nations would *not* take up every peace and security issue that arose in the world.

People who love the United Nations but do not analyze it are prone to complain that nations tend to "bypass" the organization when their vital interests are at stake. But the danger these days is not that the nations will avoid "going to the U.N." for solutions to their local and regional problems. The danger is that leaders who see political advantage in premature public debate will avoid quiet talk and regional mediation because they want to stand on that magnificent world rostrum overlooking the East River in New York and tell the world, too early and too passionately, the lurid story of their local troubles.

There is of course a value in the United Nations' safety valve role. It is good that there exists a place where every nation, large or small, can grumble for the record about its neighbors, and its neighbors have an equal opportunity to grumble in reply. But the Security Council and the General Assembly are not at their best when they are adding heat to an already overheated dispute. They function at their best as devices to record solutions arrived at by honest—which is to say, quiet—negotiation.

The growing value of the United Nations, as peace-keeper and peacemaker to the world, lies not so much in its public debates as in its operating machinery: its mediators, its observers, its inspectors, its truce supervisors, and its emergency peace-keeping forces.

The United States consistently helps build these U.N. operations for a simple and selfish reason: Their absence would require the more extensive involvement of that residual peace-keeping machinery which is the military power of the United States. If the United Nations had not been able to step in and stop the ethnic fighting on the island of Cyprus, the U.S. Sixth Fleet (which was stationed in the Mediterranean at the time) might have had to try to stop a war between Greece and Turkey, two of our NATO allies, fought with sophisticated weapons they had procured from the United States. The same kind of analysis applied in the Congo, and still applies in the Middle East. Successive Presidents of the United States have felt that if the United Nations did not take on the peace-keeping task, the United States might be forced to take a more direct hand in preventing and containing violence.

We naturally prefer to spread the risk of international peace-keeping, and most of the rest of the world also prefers that decisions about containing international violence should not all be made in one national capital. Thus, even in the cases where our force has been used most directly—in Korea, in Lebanon, in Vietnam, in the Cuba missile crisis, and in the Dominican Republic—enormous efforts have been made to associate our forces with those of other nations, and to work within doctrines and organizations that produce the widest community of political consensus.

The purpose of these exertions is precisely to avoid being drawn each time into the most costly and most dangerous way of dealing with contagious violence—which is to employ our own power in our own name.

But when an issue is "taken to the U.N.," or referred to a regional organization, or wrapped in one of the functional parcels of peace, Americans have to realize that what any international organization can do about a real problem crucially depends on what the U.S. government is willing to help it do. If, for example, we decide that in a particular case the peace-keeping job should be taken on by the United Nations, that does not reduce the load of leadership on us; it merely makes the exercise of our natural leadership more complicated.

The essence of leadership for diversity, after all, can never be the loud voice or the deceptive air of absolute certainty. Democratic leadership occurs when the leader maximizes the participation by others in the exercise of leadership. A Chinese philosopher and man of action, Lao Tse, said it all 2,500 years ago:

> . . . of a good leader, who talks little,
> When his work is done, his aim fulfilled,
> They will all say,
> "We did this ourselves!"

The Third Man

6

For two decades now, Americans have had a kind of love affair with the United Nations. The pollsters regularly turn up from 83 to 90 per cent of the American people who will endorse practically any pro-U.N. sentiment that is proferred to them by a Gallup, Roper, or Harris interviewer. Every U.S. President since 1945 and overwhelming majorities on both sides of the aisle in Congress have backed propositions to strengthen the United Nations.

The U.N. Charter was ratified in the Senate by a vote of 89 to 2—a long step from the 49 to 35 by which the Senate rejected the Covenant of the League of Nations a quarter of a century before.

The most controversial piece of U.S. legislation about the United Nations came up in 1962: the proposal to buy $100 million worth of U.N. bonds. The best political analysts in Washington gloomily predicted it would never get through Congress. But after nine months of debate, most politicians had concluded it was not safe to be caught voting against the United Nations; the authorization for a loan passed the House of Representatives by a vote of nearly 2 to 1, and the Senate by more than 3 to 1. In 1965 President Johnson asked the Senate's advice and consent to ratification of the first two amendments to the U.N. Charter, enlarging the Security Council and the Economic and Social Council to provide more room for the new nations of Asia and Africa. Again, wise and practical men were certain there would be great trouble in the Senate; and again, the opposition to the United Nations was hard to find when the votes were counted. One Senator spoke against the amendments, and left the chamber before the roll call; another Senator voted "nay," then asked unanimous consent to change his vote. That made it unanimous, 71 to 0.

The reason for this overwhelming support is that people continue to confuse the United Nations with peace. They know they are for peace, so they are for the U.N. But there is practical danger, as well as misty encouragement, in nearly universal approbation. And the most serious danger lies in the expectations of those who approve, rather than in the sour critiques of those who do not.

Political labels to one side, the vocal critics of the United Nations can be divided into two main camps: those who think the U.N. is doing too much, and those who think it is not doing enough.

One group fears an effective international organization as such; the other group fears that without a much more effective international organization, all will be lost.

At the fringe of one extreme is a doughty band of fundamentalists who look upon the United Nations as the work of a Communist conspiracy, perhaps of the Devil himself. This tiny group subsists, year in and year out, on a diet of moldy tidbits: "Alger Hiss wrote the Charter" . . . General MacArthur, in Korea, "took orders from a Russian general at the U.N." . . . and other improbable but imperishable canards.

Millions of dollars, acres of paper, tons of ink have been devoted to anti-U.N. fulminations by an impressive assortment of extremists groups. Very little of this effort is original research, and its published product contains almost no current analysis of what the United Nations is actually doing. Instead, it is mostly based on ancient and durable errors. One of these is the notion that, because a succession of Soviet citizens have held the post called Undersecretary for Political and Security Council Affairs in the U.N. Secretariat, the Russians have been in charge of every peace-keeping operation of the United Nations, including the one in the Congo. They are right in believing that the Russian members of the Secretariat are loyal, in fact and effect, to the Soviet government and not to the Secretary-General of the United Nations. But precisely for this reason, the Russians in the Secretariat are in practice bypassed on nearly all significant matters. The crucial peace-keeping operations are run out of the Secretary-General's office by a Burmese, an American, and a Guatemalan, assisted by an Indian major general.

Nevertheless, this and other stories still circulate. They seem to circulate in a narrow group, however, and it is not clear that anybody else is listening. Certainly their political effectiveness on controversial issues, when the chips are down, is close to zero.

Less frantic critics are those Americans who have learned that we cannot remain aloof from the world, but who think the alternative is somehow to run the world by the unilateral exercise of military power. This minority of militant folk is heady with leadership but has not yet come to terms with the simplest requirement of political leadership, common to every political body from the high school student council to the U.N. General Assembly. That requirement is that the leader make certain that those he leads are going where they think they want to go.

The militants say the United Nations is all right as an international debating society but should not have the capacity to do anything. Action, to these people, is the direct and unilateral use of our own armed force. They do not see that a United Nations able to keep the peace in local conflicts increases the options open to American policy makers in dealing with turbulence which can always become a threat to our own security. And they are genuinely surprised to learn that their ambition for the United Nations—that it should talk but not act—is precisely the policy of the Kremlin on U.N. affairs.

At one extreme of public opinion, then, are people who are critical of the United Nations because they fear any form of international organization, and think the only way to use our national power in our national interest is the old-fashioned method of going it alone.

The other group of critics—also small and vocal, but better informed and less profane in their correspondence than the U.N.-haters—are those who bewail the fact that the United Nations has not given us instant peace. Because they favor world peace through world organization, they are much more effective critics.

I have seen recently a well written, well designed, well printed pamphlet sponsored by a group of highly respected citizens and bearing the signature of a distinguished international lawyer. The United Nations, says the pamphlet, is a "failure." And this is so because the United Nations has not brought about:

• general and complete disarmament,
• an accepted body of comprehensive international law,
• an enforcible system of world order,
• a world legislature, and
• a world executive with a world police force to ensure compliance with its decisions.

The allegations, of course, are true—though one wonders why they are leveled at the United Nations, which was never intended to be a world government. None of its principal organizers, least of all the United States, would have signed the Charter had it been so intended.

Lacking the attributes of world government, the United Nations
—which is to say the *members* of the United Nations, acting
within the machinery of the world organization—simply have
sought to deal with the real world. It is, for better or worse, a
world where national sovereignty is still held sacred by people and
politicians; where national security is still held to rest upon national arms; where the Western concept of law is still unknown to
many and rejected by some; and where nation-states are still learning that they must act in concert on matters of common interest
but are not ready to merge national interests in a universal
union.

If the fundamentalist U.N.-haters are living in a past that never
was, the dedicated writers of ideal constitutions are dreaming of a
future too far down the corridors of time to have much bearing on
the world as it is.

The attitude of the rest of us—the 83 to 90 per cent of Americans who think the United Nations is the best start we have toward
world order—is readily described: We are stalwart but vague.
There are dangers in that stance.

One danger is that a warm feeling about the United Nations is
not a very dependable source of wisdom and courage in moments
of crisis.

I shall not soon forget the political shock wave produced in our
politics by the Congo crisis when Americans suddenly discovered
that soldiers on a peace-keeping mission sometimes had to shoot
back at people who insisted on shooting at the peace-keepers. It
was more comfortable to think of "peace" as a cartoonist's image,
a vaguely female figure in a pure white gown, mouthing sweet
nothings and clutching her olive branch. But when this ethereal
creature, adjusting her halo to a rakish angle, whipped out her six-
shooter to defend her right to walk a policeman's beat on the
streets of Elisabethville, most Americans did a double take. It took
several months for the usually dependable pro-U.N. organizations
to decide, and convince their constituencies, that what was wrong

with the Congo picture was not the U.N. actions (or U.S. support of them), but their own previous notion that international peace-keeping could somehow be carried on without anybody getting killed.

The other danger of widespread but vague approval is that it gives rise to an unrealistic expectation that the United Nations can suddenly take on a task which the requisite majority of its members do not yet feel is theirs to tackle. Some of the same people who criticized the United Nations for being forceful in Katanga later demanded indignantly that the U.N. teach a forceful lesson to those who resisted its mandate in Cyprus. And our domestic debate over the Vietnam war has been strewn with proposals for the United Nations to do forceful things for which there was no majority and no money.

Yet, despite the perils of vagueness, there are worse fates than widespread approval for a government policy. Over the past few years we have gradually poured more content, more understanding of the practical realities, into our unwavering support for the purposes of the United Nations. These purposes have not lost their political pull: betterment of the human condition still retains a certain popularity. But the approbation now covers a record of action, too.

The United Nations has become a major issue in American politics because people have come to realize that what the United Nations does really matters, and had therefore better be watched as carefully as we have long since learned to watch the policies and actions of major national governments.

The Korean war was controversial enough. But that war, in which we fought under a U.N. flag as the U.N.'s executive agent for aims prescribed in U.N. resolutions, was nevertheless viewed by most Americans as essentially an American show. Now, after several generations of talk about organizing world peace and enforcing the rule of law, three really significant peace-keeping forces of a truly international character have been placed and maintained in the field. Five thousand men, drawn from seven countries, kept watch over the Gaza Strip and the Israeli-Egyptian frontier; 20,000 men, drawn from 21 countries, patrolled and periodically fought for four years in the Congo; 6,000 men, drawn from six countries, sat on the lid in Cyprus. Each of these missions was backed by a U.S. Air Force airlift; the Congo lift was the longest and largest such operation in the history of military aviation, moving 76,000 soldiers and 14,000 tons of military cargo with high professional skill and no serious accident.

The United Nations is thus a proper subject for political controversy because it is doing more things, on a larger scale, more vital to our national interests, than ever before—and because the going is getting rough. Peace-keeping turns out to be practical, but it is also hard on the nerves.

As the practice of peace moves from oratory to operations, we have learned some important things about the business. The most important lesson, I think, is the need for an international "third man" always on tap, to negotiate the cessation of fighting, to help settle disputes, and to arrange for change that will avoid violence if possible.

In world affairs this third party may be an international debating forum, a system of mediation, a team of on-the-ground inspectors, a police force—or just an individual diplomat shuttling anonymously from one disputant to another, trying to find a basis for getting them together. The "third man" need not be the United Nations; he can be sponsored by any of the pluralistic parcels into which the peace is divided. But in a growing number of dangerous and intractable disputes the "man in the middle" comes from the United Nations.

It started with Greece in 1946. The Greeks complained about foreign aid to rebel guerrillas, and a U.N. Peace Observation Commission was sent to help the Greek government stabilize the country and hold supervised elections.

In 1948, the British mandate expired in Palestine. To keep peace after the partition, U.N. truce supervisors and mixed armistice commissions were placed around the borders of Israel. They have kept a taut and precarious peace there for seventeen years, and their technique is simple: Be there. I had occasion to watch from Washington the chronology of a retaliatory raid by Israel on an illegal Syrian gun emplacement on a hill above the Sea of Galilee. The fighting started at midnight; the peace-keepers were there, in their white jeeps with the blue flags, by 3 A.M.; a cease-fire had been negotiated, and was in effect, by 7:30 the same morning.

Also in 1948, the partition of India and Pakistan left a residue of rivalry over the status of Kashmir, an issue of enormous bitterness since Hindus and Moslems had been murdered by the millions in communal fighting during the previous year. A courageous U.N. general from Australia, with an international team of military observers, still administers that precarious Kashmir armistice line; after the fracas of September 1965, a Canadian general assembled yet another peace-keeping force to patrol other parts of the long India-Pakistan frontier. An American mediator, also working for the United Nations, has commuted fruitlessly to the area. The Security Council wearily debates the issue once or twice a year. As this is written Kashmir has erupted again, and no settlement is in sight. But even if Kashmir continues to poison the politics of the subcontinent, it must be said that seventeen years of precarious cease-fire has been better than a renewal of communal mayhem, and the United Nations merits full marks for keeping it that way for so long.

In 1950, the Republic of Korea was invaded and a large armed force under delegated command was organized to repel the invasion. American troops were the core of this command, and 54,246 of them were killed defending the Charter's central principle that in a civilized world nations should band together to stop aggression.

In 1956, the United Nations arranged a cease-fire when Israel,

France, and the United Kingdom attacked the Sinai Desert and the Suez Canal. With the United States and the Soviet Union sharing an interest in getting the fighting stopped, a U.N. Emergency Force was quickly agreed on, and was rushed to the danger spots. It was still there nine years later.

In 1958, a special session of the General Assembly sent a U.N. observer to Lebanon in response to the Lebanese government's complaint that foreign infiltrators were trying to overturn it. The United States had already sent in some troops of its own as a holding action; they withdrew when the United Nations took over. Conditions were rapidly stabilized, U.N.-supervised elections were held, and the threat to orderly government evaporated.

In 1960, in the Congo, an army mutiny within hours of the independence celebration brought the United Nations to its largest and most controversial peace-keeping task. Four years and three unsuccessful secessions later, the United Nations withdrew its troops leaving a parliament, the beginnings of an effective government, and the elements of federal order. It will take many years for the Congolese to learn to govern effectively; but they would not have had a large and potentially prosperous nation to experiment in if the United Nations had not by its presence prevented a direct confrontation between East and West in the heart of Africa.

In 1962, a U.N. mediator helped avert a war over the future of West New Guinea and a U.N. Special Representative, supported by a battalion of Pakistani troops, administered the transition of that territory from Dutch to Indonesian rule.

And in 1963-1964, fighting between ethnic Greeks and Turks on the island of Cyprus almost led three times to a war between Greece and Turkey. Only the quick dispatch of Scandinavian, Irish, and Canadian troops to join the British in a U.N. force got the situation under control, and kept it quiet for the tense months that followed.

This inventory covers only the major operations in which military personnel had to be used. There are many other cases. The

United Nations played a third-party role when the Soviets remained in Iran after World War II; when the Dutch and Indonesians were fighting in the Far East; when Lebanon and then Jordan entered complaints against the United Arab Republic; when Thailand and Cambodia threatened to go to war to settle sovereignty over a temple on their common border; and in a good many other incipient disputes which never made the headlines because nobody got killed.

The clearest lesson from the catalogue of U.N. crises is that each is different from all the rest. Threats to the peace can, and do, break out almost anywhere. In the past two decades, major peacekeeping operations have been undertaken by the United Nations four times in the Middle East, three times in Southern Europe, twice in Southeast Asia, and once each in the Far East, in the Western Pacific, in Central Africa, and on a Mediterranean island. In the Western Hemisphere, the Security Council has had peace and security crises on its docket fourteen times, though action to send observers was taken only in the 1965 Dominican case. As this is written the Security Council has exactly fifty-seven varieties of large and small disputes listed on its agenda, some of them dangerous enough to require an active watching brief by the "third man" in international politics.

There used to be much talk of a U.N. standing force to keep the peace. But it is hard to conceive an international standing force that could carry out the variety of political and military tasks which the real world thrusts upon the world organization. In each of the thirteen alarms to which the United Nations has responded with some kind of "peace-keeping operation"—the accepted euphemism for military force used by an international organization —the military and political problem to be solved was different, and required a different mix of nationalities, skin colors, political orientation, weaponry, and military skills. Colored troops could not be readily used in Cyprus; an all-white U.N. force would have been a disaster in the Congo. During the early rounds of fighting in

Katanga, it was assumed that a peace-keeping force did not need air support; as a result, the U.N. force, representing the majesty of the world community, was pinned down for several weeks by a single Fuga Magister fighter, the slowest jet airplane on the military market, piloted by a couple of white adventurers.

The ground, naval, and air forces potentially needed for any emergency, anywhere in the world, would be so enormous, and would require such a large airlift capability and therefore an international base system, that the members of the United Nations would certainly refuse to pay to have it sit around awaiting the next threat to the peace. Instead, we have developed by trial and error a "flexible call-up system," whereby countries willing to participate in international peace-keeping earmark some of their own armed forces for United Nations service, and make them available, if necessary overnight, to meet a particular emergency. In this system the crucial role of the United States has been to get the peace-keepers to the area of trouble in a hurry. Within less than twenty-four hours after a cease-fire was reached in the Suez case, Swedish troops had been transported from Sweden to the banks of the Suez Canal. Similarly in the Congo, U.N. troops from Tunisia were on the ground in Leopoldville less than a day after the Security Council passed the first enabling resolution.

Not so very long ago a nation in some remote corner of the world could start an aggression and months would pass before the rest of the world caught up with what was going on. As the world shrinks, so does the time available for unpublicized military operations. Today, with nearly instantaneous communications around the world, it is almost impossible to hide an aggression for more than a few hours. Breaches of the peace can now be kept under the lights of international observation—if some agent of the world community is there, able and willing to switch on the lights.

It is not easy to single out the man who invented a great idea at a critical moment in a long negotiation. But when the history of mankind's best and most durable effort to build an international order is written down, by historians who survived to write it because the generation that split the atom apart discovered how to weld the world together, it will surely identify as the Founding Father of modern international peace-keeping Lester Pearson of Canada.

Lester Pearson received the Nobel Peace Prize for proposing the rapid establishment, with the consent of the nations concerned, of an emergency international U.N. force to secure and supervise the cessation of hostilities in Suez in early November 1956. What he thus proposed in Canada's name (at the suggestion of a momentarily self-effacing U.S. delegation to the United Nations) was a truly creative act—in its own way quite as creative as the acts of Richard Arkwright or Orville Wright or Enrico Fermi. Like other great perceptions in the pell-mell advance of civilization, Pearson's act was a piece of political alchemy; it combined deep understanding of fundamental historical trends with an intuitive sense of the right moment to take the next step.

It is appropriate for Canada to be recorded in a place of honor in the modern history of peace, for Canada has a nearly perfect record of participating in peace-keeping enterprises, exceeding even the notable score of the dependable Swedes. Except in West New Guinea, where one country provided all the U.N. policemen, Canada has assigned Canadians to every peace-keeping operation of the United Nations, and has also served for more than a decade as a member of the International Control Commissions in Laos and Vietnam. Canadians have jounced in white jeeps along the sensitive borders of Israel, policed the tender armistice line in Kashmir, fought and died for collective security in Korea, zipped up the Sinai borders after Suez, helped extinguish the Lebanon fuse two years later, helped prevent secession in the Congo two years after that, and two years later again were assigned to the dusty wastes of Arabia to observe the abortive cease-fire in Yemen. When the Cyprus feud became an international fight, Canada sent her famed Van Doos, the Royal 22nd Regiment, to account for one-sixth of the U.N. Force there; as often happens, the Canadians got there first, in their own planes at their own expense, and were promptly assigned to the hottest sector on the island, the notorious Kyrenia Pass.

The Canadians have learned much from this experience, and so have the military personnel from all the other countries contributing troops to one or another U.N. operation—54 nations, including fifteen nations born since the Charter was signed. They have learned from experience that an international police force has a mission unlike most national military missions, usually less military and always less national. And the most useful lessons about its nature come out of the United Nations' four-year ordeal in the Congo.

The whole story of the Congo is a jumbled tale. It has elements of finance and economics and politics, domestic and international varieties; it presents examples of fumbling and examples of superb performance; it has chapters on propaganda, on knavery, and on promises made and broken; it has stories of patience, persistence, valor, and success; it has moments of violence and periods of diplomacy.

And it has its share of human tragedy.

On January 3, 1963, in the outskirts of Jadotville, U.N. soldiers fired a volley at a civilian automobile which apparently ignored a signal to halt and tried to evade a search point. The woeful result was the death of two women riding in the car. A dramatic photograph of the anguished and wounded driver, husband of one of the women, told this tragic story on the front pages of our newspapers. Journalistically, it was a great photograph, and I suspect we shall see it again because it might well win a prize some day.

But the horror of that single mistake by a nervous soldier with a gun in his hand almost obscured what had just happened in Jadotville that day. A brave, professional, and disciplined Indian general, in command of a tiny U.N. detachment, had made a brilliant sortie in an open jeep and talked his way into Jadotville without firing a shot—with the assistance of the town mayor, who preferred U.N. protection to dependence on undisciplined Katangese troops and desperate mercenaries who had vowed to fight for the town "block by block," destroying its industrial facilities in the process.

There is no acceptable reason why those two women had to die in the outskirts of Jadotville. The danger is that the tragic side may be all that is remembered, along with unpaid assessments, recriminations among allies, and Soviet attacks on the U.N. Secretariat. If this happens, we shall ignore one of the brightest chapters in the history of international cooperation.

Members of U.N. peace-keeping forces are soldiers from the military establishments of the nations contributing units. They are commanded by professional military officers. They wear uniforms and carry guns. They sleep in tents or barracks and eat military rations. But once they put on the blue beret, or if need be the blue helmet, they find they are supposed to be soldiers without enemies, fighters without rancor, members of an armed force without a military objective—their mission not to start shooting but to stop it, not to win a battle but to see to it there is no battle to be won or lost.

The implications that flow from this strange state of affairs for soldiers-turned-peacemakers are large and fascinating. In a remote section of the Congo, during 1962, I visited with a brigadier general from Malaysia, commanding a Malayan U.N. brigade. In a real war, he said, he would be merely commanding a brigade, but with the U.N. force he had to command each platoon. His point was that the smallest incident in the life of a minor patrol can easily become a major political issue. In the jungles of Malaya, the Communists who had been shooting at these same soldiers were clearly the enemy—no doubt about it. "But here," said the brigadier, "if somebody shoots at our soldiers, it is a political question whether they could even shoot back."

The point was clear enough in the case of Indian troops manning a checkpoint who were attacked by a howling mob of several thousand women organized by secessionists under Moise Tshombe. The women kicked, spat, slapped, ripped shirts, and tore insignia from the stoic Gurkhas who had been ordered not to fight even in self-defense. As the women began to tire of this one-sided fight, the Indians fired exactly nine rounds of ammunition over their heads and advanced to disperse the mob, using only their batons. The Indian officer in charge told me that an army unit brought in to put down such an outbreak under what he called "normal" conditions could readily have caused dozens or scores of civilian deaths.

One commander in the Congo said that when opposing troops run from a police force, the "non-enemy" principle may require the U.N. force to let them get away. Curiously enough, he did not think this was necessarily a military disadvantage. "If a man has to run away from you," he said with a grin, "he will deliberately exaggerate the size and effectiveness of your force, in order to look better in the eyes of his own people."

If the rank and file of a peace-keeping force have to make a difficult adjustment, so do the officers. The commander of a peace force often must go out ahead of his troops. This used to be standard operating practice in ancient China, and in Europe of the Middle Ages. A commander would ride out to parley with the opposing commander, to see whether things could be settled without anybody getting hurt. In more modern warfare, the commanding officer doesn't spend much time in no-man's-land. But in this sense, U.N. peace-keeping has brought the sensible Middle Ages up to date—for the object, once again, is to pacify.

The brigadier commanding the Indian brigade in the Congo made a regular and successful practice of going out ahead of his troops and persuading hostile local forces to return stolen helicopters, retire gracefully from the field without battle, and even give up cities. It is remarkable, the brigadier reported, how well this method works in situations where the other side is not quite sure of itself or its orders. "If you do something that looks deliberately stupid, it is sometimes so surprising to others that you get away with it."

A final distinction between an international peace force and a conventional military one is that peace-keepers in an underdeveloped area are often drawn deeply into the civil life of the community. United Nations units in the Congo found themselves providing leadership, supplies, transportation, and other services to local governments, and sometimes to private firms, in an effort to help the economy get moving again. The U.N. force even had to develop a scale of charges by which businesses could be billed for hauling goods to market in U.N. military vehicles.

Soldiers without enemies, operating on behalf of the world community, are a new kind of people doing a new kind of work. Their doctrine, their mandate, their training manuals, are still first drafts—and not yet ready for final printing.

The U.N. spectaculars in the Middle East, the Congo, and Cyprus have helped Americans look at the United Nations as a practical political organization—neither a Holy Grail nor a compact with Satan, but an instrument of American foreign policy, somewhat complicated by the fact that it is an instrument of the national foreign policies of more than a hundred other nations. If there are fewer people today who regard the U.N. system with the sentiments one might reserve for his favorite charity, there are also fewer who see in its every act the hand of dark conspiracy directed at themselves. Americans instead are beginning to accept the United Nations as a limited but vital working part of international diplomacy, one which deserves to be taken seriously and examined with professional care.

How much further can, or should, the United Nations develop its peace-keeping capacity? It is a fair question—but no answer today has much chance of making sense tomorrow.

For the United Nations has whatever capacity its members can agree to endow it with at any given time for any given purpose. Secretary-General U Thant once said that his executive role is to be guided by the decisions of the relevant U.N. bodies. That is a rather restricted and formalistic way for an executive to view his capacity for independent initiatives; and U Thant's actions, like Dag Hammarskjold's, go farther than his words. Yet it is still broadly true that until one knows the nature of an emergency, and then plumbs the will of the United Nations' majority to act in the face of common danger, no man can say what the "capacity" of the U.N. is to act in defense of the peace.

The day before the Korean invasion, the day before the Suez crisis, the day before the army mutiny in the Congo, nobody would have dreamed that the United Nations would take on the peace-keeping tasks it did in fact assume. Its capacity is the sum of the wills of its members to act together.

Dag Hammarskjold once said it well: "The basic policy line for this organization is that the United Nations simply must respond to those demands which must be made of it . . . the United Nations should respond and should have confidence in its strength and capacity to respond."

There is always the question of how much of an administrative load can safely be taken on. There is, too, the sticky and contentious problem of finance, and there is the always difficult matter of getting first-rate people capable of doing unprecedented jobs in a fog of controversy and frustration. The U.N.'s small operations in Greece, Palestine, and Kashmir helped put it in training to climb what Hammarskjold called "the very steep hill of Suez"; in turn, the operation in the Gaza Strip served as calisthenics for the Congo, and what was learned in the Congo deeply affected the mandate, the strategy, and the tactics of the Cyprus operation.

But the lesson from thirteen alarms—that each peace-keeping task is without precedent—means the United Nations' resources are never fixed or exhaustible. Being busy in one place must not preclude getting busy if necessary in another place.

The measure of future U.N. actions for peace is not some predetermined "capacity to act," but rather the complex circumstances under which the requisite majority of its members can agree to pool their strength and act together for the Charter's purposes. The real variable in the equation is not the age of the organization, nor the state of its bank account, nor the level of its current work load. It is the politics of consent.

There are, fortunately, two sides to the politics of consent. It does limit the growth of international peace-keeping. At the same time it spurs the growth of those scientific and technical forms of cooperation that are making the world one, whether the world's political leaders like it or not. What science has done for international comity is worth a chapter of its own.

The Impact of Discovery

7

Given enough perspective, the world we live in is evidently a lovely place. Listen to the only men who have been far enough away from earth to see it whole.

"What a beautiful view." Those were the first words of Astronaut Shepard, the first countryman of ours to look down from outer space. Cosmonaut Titov was of the same mind: "Our earth is wonderful, the blue halo around it is very beautiful." Listen to Cosmonaut Nikolayev: "Our planet is uncommonly beautiful and looks wonderful from cosmic heights." And to the immediate reaction of Astronaut McDivitt from Gemini 4, when he first looked out and exclaimed: "Beautiful . . . beautiful! It looks great up here!"

This new fraternity of spacemen speaks not of nations, of continents, of islands, but of our earth, our planet, our world. They neglect to mention its divisions, but find it whole and blue and beautiful.

Suppose a Martian or Venusian said to one of our astronauts, on first encounter, "Tell me, in a few words, what's the essence of what you on earth have learned from your brief half-million years' experience with life?" Would our man try to explain to Mars and Venus the sordid aggressions, the border disputes, the issues in the Cold War? Or would he talk about what we have learned, with much stalling and much grinding of our political gears, about how groups of men can cooperate with each other?

I think our astronaut would be more likely than most Americans to talk about international cooperation. For he operates under an Act of Congress which enjoins NASA to conduct its space program in cooperation with other nations. He knows that every shot from Cape Kennedy requires a web of interlocking agreements with three dozen other lands. And he would know, too, that an international agreement in the works would obligate any nation into whose territory he might fall to return him to his country of origin, in return for our agreement, and the Soviets', to assume the liability for accidents caused by experiments in outer space.

He might even know that in 1961, Year Five of the Age of Space, the United States proposed, the Soviets co-sponsored, and the U.N. General Assembly unanimously voted a landmark resolution on the law of outer space. By this resolution, space and celestial bodies have been placed beyond the claim of individual nations. We have all agreed that the principles of the U.N. Charter should apply to men from earth no matter how far they get from home.

This does not mean that outer space cannot be used for military purposes. Freedom of the high seas permits destroyers and submarines and aircraft carriers to pursue missions that are presumed to be peaceable in the absence of an aggressive act. Freedom of outer space means about the same thing: Defensive deployment of vehicles such as observation satellites is no violation of international law or the U.N. Charter, and is therefore a "peaceful use" within the meaning of the General Assembly resolution.

We do not yet know whether the Charter's principles will commend themselves to whatever intelligence our envoys may meet Out There. But the preamble and the first two articles of the Charter are a good summary of what we have learned from several thousand years of feuding and fighting among men who are brothers, and brothers who are different from each other.

The law of outer space is like the law of your own community: Your freedom and my freedom to do damage to others is restrained in the interest of my freedom and your freedom to walk unmolested in the streets we share. There is no other basis for freedom with civil order, whether in Missouri or the moon. So if we do meet anybody in outer space, and he or she is intelligent, the logic of this concentrated wisdom may turn out to have galactic appeal.

The exploration of outer space has actually drawn men and nations together more than it has split them apart. The same is true, as we shall see, of Antarctica, that empty windy land populated by penguins who know how to picket but have not learned to carry signs. One lesson of this analogy is that it is easier to cooperate where there are no people. But a more relevant lesson is surely this: When nations perceive a common interest, they can readily come to clear and enforcible agreements.

The current effort to organize our world according to Charter principles began, not with the atom bomb but with the earlier determination by a few men in Washington that World War II should not produce as transitory a peace settlement as World War I. The first American work on postwar planning was actually done before the United States entered the war, and the first formal step toward establishing the United Nations system of organizations came in the early summer of 1943.

President Franklin D. Roosevelt was mindful of the stricture of John Maynard Keynes, that the failure of Versailles and the League of Nations was due to the lack of concrete "ideas . . . for clothing with the flesh of life the commandments which [Woodrow Wilson] had thundered from the White House." That is why Roosevelt early developed the principle (which he practiced but never preached) that an ultimate pattern of peace must be put together over a period of time out of its major fragments. It was too much, he felt, to build a peace all at once, in a single stroke of diplomacy, from such a ruin as World War II might make of the world.

In the early months of postwar planning, therefore, the planning was in bits and pieces, reaching into every specialized corner of the government. The dynamics of specialist enthusiasm would be used to provide motive power for building the peace, out of building blocks which would take the form of international organizations for special as well as general purposes, for technical as well as political functions.

Thus, over in the Treasury Department, the first planning papers that were to lead to the Bretton Woods Conference, and later the World Bank and Monetary Fund, were drafted early in the war. Across town in the Public Health Service, doctors dreamed of a World Health Organization.

Elsewhere university people began talking about a world education agency. The labor movement worked hard to preserve the International Labor Organization, temporarily exiled from Geneva to Montreal. The forecasters of weather, already organized for almost seventy years in an international organization, began the rethinking that found expression in the World Meteorological Organization.

As a neophyte in government employed in the Department of Agriculture, I remember working on postwar food planning in 1941, several months before the United States was actually engaged in fighting the war we assumed from the first would be won.

We can see now that it was clearly a good thing for the pattern of peace to develop in a fragmented way. It was much easier to reach international agreement in the relatively "safe," relatively non-political subjects with which the U.N.'s Specialized Agencies deal. The world of the 1940s and 1950s was far from ready for an enforcible peace system, and progress in one field of endeavor could not be made to depend on simultaneous progress in all the others.

The unanswerable reason for creating each international organization—adding another fragment to a world pattern for peace—has been the progress of science and technology. Whenever the scientists achieve a breakthrough in what can be done by man for man, it suddenly seems outrageous not to be channeling the new power that new knowledge confers upon us.

Before we knew that mosquitoes carried malaria, and before we knew how to murder mosquitoes with DDT, nobody thought about eradicating malaria from the face of the earth, because it could not be done. Now that we know it can be done, we are well on our way toward the doing of it—even if the task proves to be somewhat longer, and the mosquitoes somewhat more resistant to our attempts to poison them, than the scientists thought when they proudly swept every anopheles from the island of Sardinia just after World War II.

Before there was radio, we did not need to have a large standing international conference to divide up the frequency spectrum; now, the International Telecommunications Union is just that. Before there were airplanes flying across frontiers and oceans, we did not need an International Civil Aviation Organization. Today we have international agreements on aerial navigation because the alternative would be mayhem compounded.

Thus every new scientific invention, every technological innovation, seems to require the invention of a new international program to contain, channel, and control it. A precept of American business is that necessity is the mother of invention. But in the business of diplomacy, the reverse is true as well: Invention is the mother of necessity.

Sometimes this technological imperative is in curious contrast to the alarums and excursions of political rivalries among nations. Ever since the Bolshevik Revolution the United States and the Soviet Union have been working together in the hunting of seals in the Bering Sea, simply because it makes sense to do so, Cold War or no. Ever since the early 1930s the Turks and the Russians have maintained an annual joint cattle market, even while Stalin was claiming the very areas of Turkey where the cattle are raised and sold.

Perhaps the clearest case of the technological imperative is the extraordinary cooperation among the scientists who explore the frozen continent of Antarctica. It can serve us here to illustrate an international bargain that really works for all the parties to it.

We think of the South Pole and its environs as an enormous cake of ice, with no known resources worth digging down to find. But Antarctica is one end of the earth's magnet. Impulses fed into the magnetic field down there are flung far into space to return with nearly undiminished energy at the Magnetic North Pole, in Canada; this may turn out to be of prime importance in the development of international telecommunications.

In the enormous Antarctic freezer, moreover, samples of space particles that have bombarded this planet in past ages are preserved. The particles can be dated by their position in the snow layers, and by radioactive techniques. If studies show that these particles have a recurring pattern, we may some day be able to predict what our astronauts will run into as they travel through outer space.

The seas around the Antarctic continent are the source of all the major ocean currents around the globe. The Antarctic waters are peculiar, it seems, in that turbulent vertical currents sweep from the ocean bed to the surface, tearing loose the rare and elemental nutrients necessary to sustain life, and then transporting them along the ocean currents to all the other seas of the world. The Antarctic oceans may therefore be the main source of all life in the sea, and thus of all the marine foods of which man now extracts only a tiny fraction.

The dividends from research into these matters are important to the national interest of dozens of countries. Fourteen of them are curious enough, and well enough endowed with competent scientists, to do some exploring in Antarctica. They are doing it in cooperation because they perceive that competition would make the job harder, slower, and more expensive. The story of how this eminently sensible conclusion was reached is little known, and worth the telling.

Long before the enormous scientific potential of Antarctica was guessed, the curiosity of Americans and other peoples was sniffing at the edges of its forbidding terrain. One hundred and fifty years ago our whalers and sealers were among the first to penetrate the forbidding oceans of the Antarctic. Later, Rear Admirals Charles Wilkes and Richard E. Byrd led the way to discovery of the continent and the early probes into its interior. Today the scientists, and those who make it possible for them to get there and stay there, live and work in stations spotted from the edges of the continent to the South Pole.

But Antarctica has never been a private domain. Other nations pursued programs similar to our own. Some of them even established territorial claims to wedges of the Antarctic pie. Access to the frozen continent was attracting more and more scientists and explorers, and began to be an issue in international politics.

In 1957 and 1958, the International Geophysical Year threatened to convert the national rivalries into troublesome confrontations of power and prestige. Twelve countries mounted IGY expeditions to Antarctica. The always touchy question of sovereignty—who could come into which part of the icy waste —became acute. And as the fringes of the continent began to see ships and airplanes, more and more people feared that this vast uncharted area might become the site of military installations designed to alter the world balance of power.

It was these latent fears and potential troubles which led to one of the most sensible treaties in the not always rational history of international diplomacy. The Antarctic Treaty, signed on December 1, 1959, and ratified by the United States on August 18, 1960, was an innovation without precedent on the world's land surface.

Essentially, the treaty applied to the whole southern end of the globe, south of 60° south latitude. Its doctrine is simple: that all nations would have access to Antarctica, as long as that access was for peaceful scientific purposes.

The treaty obligates the fourteen treaty partners to cooperate with each other in scientific investigation. It prohibits military activities, and forbids nuclear explosions; it was, among other things, history's first nuclear test ban agreement. It authorizes any signatory nation to inspect the activities of all other nations in Antarctica.

For the United States, as the nation with the greatest capability to mount and support scientific investigations in Antarctica, this treaty was clearly better than limiting ourselves to one slice of a much divided pie. As things stand, we are at liberty to investigate anywhere, build anywhere, fly anywhere, traverse anywhere in this vast and still mysterious Southland.

The treaty did not set up an international organization as such. Every year or two, the nations meet and recommend measures to improve the treaty's operation. Twenty-six measures from three such meetings have already been approved by governments since the treaty went into force in June 1961.

The nations operating in Antarctica have agreed, for example, to exchange detailed reports about their expeditions. The inspections called for by the treaty have actually been carried through; we have sent inspectors to the installations of a number of our Antarctic partners, including the Soviet Union. And we have opened our own peaceful stations to their scrutiny whenever they care to come.

The United States has given and received help from almost every other country active in Antarctica. Many a life has been saved, and many an expedition completed, because of timely help across national lines made invisible by the realities of human hardship and the prospect of scientific gain.

Outside the Antarctic continent itself, the same cooperative spirit prevails. For example, our advance base for Antarctica is actually at Christchurch in New Zealand, and we provide logistic support for some of New Zealand's operations in Antarctica.

Even in the formal meetings of the treaty powers, national delegations are impressed to see a spirit of accommodation seldom matched in the meetings of other international bodies. There are heated discussions, and national positions defined with vigor; but the debaters are more bent on achieving a constructive purpose which all regard as common. Here, at least, even Communists cooperate with a will; for in the land of ice and penguins, discoveries by any nation are a gain for all.

A hundred other examples could be cited to show that there need be nothing woolly-headed or misty-eyed about international technological cooperation in the remaining third of the twentieth century. Disorderly, yes. Impractical, no. An alliance of man to cope with his environment begins to look like plain common sense.

All ideologies are equally opposed to such common enemies as rinderpest, winter wheat rust, and the tsetse fly. It has long been clear that everybody gains and nobody loses if enough nations agree to stop polluting the seas with oil, if they investigate together the tropic mysteries of the Indian Ocean, or if they pool their purses and personnel to stamp out smallpox and typhus and yellow fever and yaws.

It is noticeable that men of science can often "speak the same language," even through an interpreter; that physicians can cooperate with each other in a global war on disease; that farmers can teach each other how to get higher yields without politics getting too much in the way. The vocabulary of science has its own peculiarities, its own myopias, its own oversimplifications. But when scientists talk across national frontiers their conversation, on their own subjects, is often mercifully free of the semantic distortions imposed by political ideology, economic dogma, and the conventional wisdom of crusty cultures.

This is all good, but it is not enough. The spawning of new technologies is not all beneficent. The technology of atomic fission and fusion can provide electric power for national development; it can also incinerate all life in the Northern Hemisphere.

The parochialism of each major field of knowledge is not necessarily an improvement on the more familiar parochialism of nation-states, *unless* the demonstration of experts working with each other on food and health leads in fact to nations working with each other to keep the general peace.

A civilization which guarantees people enough to eat and longer life, and then exposes them to lethal radioactivity, is not moving onward and upward. It is moving sidewise toward a precipice. So the ultimate worth of every specialized or functional body must be measured partly by whether it helps develop the general or political bodies charged with peaceful solution of international conflicts. Every step to strengthen the Specialized Agencies of the United Nations must in conscience be matched with steps to control arms and develop the peace-keeping machinery of the U.N. organization itself. For if a workable pattern of peace must be constructed patiently by building first its component parts, the parts in the end must fit a pattern that makes enough sense to keep us not only fed and healthy but also alive. This is the mandate laid upon the administrators, the builders of human institutions, by what Robert Oppenheimer has called the "thundering impact of discovery upon society."

"Men are social by nature," said Pope John XXIII in *Pacem in Terris,* that extraordinary document so full of universal truths.

"Since men are social by nature, they are meant to live with others and to work for one another's welfare." And hence, Pope John wrote a few paragraphs later, "the whole reason for the existence of civil authorities is the realization of the common good."

The international realization of the common good is no visionary proposition. A community of working world institutions is already a fact of modern life. From around the world comes a constructive clamor: the noises of a world community a-building under our noses.

It is anything but a tidy sight. The world community has no master plan, and no foreseeable ultimate shape. Few of its structures are yet complete, and many have not even been started. Its law is in a primitive stage of evolution, and lawbreakers still abound. The police and fire departments of the world community are primitive and unreliable, too. And the world's school system still has more dropouts than stay-ins.

Yet there is work in progress. Around most of the world, most of the peoples—even as they hold to their weapons and cling to their disputes—have picked up tools in cooperative labors. In the course of it all, knowledge is diffused and technology spreads by contagion, indifferent to cultural differences, making incentive systems and decentralization and looseness of organization as inevitable as central heating and indoor plumbing. Standards are set, and regulations are published, and international law—which is more and more the practice of international organizations—grows in the way law grows best: organically.

Our considerable experience tells us that three conditions have to be fulfilled before nations can agree to work together—even if they continue to argue vigorously about why they are working together.

First, the technology to make cooperation necessary has to be there. But technology does not speak for itself. So, *second,* national leaders who understand its promise and its peril must come to feel the need to cooperate, to channel and contain the inventions of the scientists and the innovations of the engineers.

We see again and again that a nation can perceive its own interest in cooperating with others about one subject, while carrying on political quarrels on other subjects. In dealing with other men, it is hard for us to trust them in compartments, to sign an agreement on one subject and fight with them or haul them into court on another subject. Yet that is just what nations do, because technology makes it imperative.

There must, *third,* be international institutions to reflect these common interests—to put the technology in the service of felt needs.

Let us use one example to bring these abstractions down to earth, or at least as far down as the atmosphere that envelops the earth.

What is happening to international weather reporting and forecasting is both clear and exciting. Beyond that, what man might do to modify the weather makes a political scientist blink at the social fallout of the atmospheric sciences. That cliché of Mark Twain's is obsolescent: Somebody *is* doing something about the weather.

Men have always known that their livelihood, and often their lives, depended upon the weather; but until recently that was nearly all they knew of it. They endowed the elements with the attributes of gods. You may have seen the lovely Tower of the Winds built in Athens in the first or second century B.C., or the sculptures of the fierce Rain God of the Maya civilization in Mexico, or the Pueblo Indian dance to appease the Sun God. In any event, the chances are that in the past twenty-four hours you have uttered or heard some superstition that comes to us out of the rich mythology about weather still deep in our culture.

Until recently the best a sailor could do about the weather was to wet his finger, watch the sky, and repeat the inherited folk wisdom: "Red sky at morning, sailor take warning; red sky at night, sailor's delight." Some farmers who lived close to the earth acquired—as a function of their joints if not of their reason— mysterious and often misleading hunches about the weather. The hunches did not help very much; the rain still fell before the hay was in, and the ground was still parched and dustblown when the sun shone too hot for too long.

What did help were the first steps in the transition from mythology to technology.

In the middle of the seventeenth century one of Galileo's graduate assistants developed a primitive barometer. In the early eighteenth century, Fahrenheit, in Holland, invented the mercury thermometer. As such instruments were built, the continuous curiosity of men led to the beginnings of a systematic science of the atmosphere.

For a while there were some rudimentary tools but no theory to work with. Then in the nineteenth century the physicist Helmholtz worked out the basic theoretical equations of hydrodynamics, but nobody knew how to apply the theory to the way the atmosphere actually worked. For much of the next century, theory ran ahead of tools in the newly emerging science of meteorology.

Suddenly, new inventions came along rapidly. The electric telegraph made it possible to collect enough data fast enough to make the first stab at forecasting the weather without depending on old wives' tales or plying the gods with questions. Then came the radio—and the airplane—and photo transmission by wireless. World War II came, also, with its suddenly expanded and urgent requirements for greatly extended upper air observations. And the new electronic computers came to revolutionize every field of science.

Soon the science of meteorology was coming of age due to the convergence of three major developments.

One was a refinement and simplification of Helmholtz's theories of hydrodynamics and their application to the atmosphere. Meteorologists came to understand much more about the physical processes occurring in the upper air. They could begin building more complex models of the earth's atmosphere as a basis for long-term weather forecasting.

When observation and communication satellites came along,

they offered the potential for collecting enough data, from enough parts of the world's atmosphere, to sample the wind and weather all around the globe, instead of depending on inadequate observations in a tenth of the necessary places.

Then the electronic computer opened the prospect of processing enough data fast enough to make longer-term forecasting mechanically possible before the weather had come and gone.

The marriage of all these new technologies made it possible for the first time to think seriously about the atmosphere of the earth as the single, self-contained physical system it is now considered to be. With the technology as well as the theory in sight, the weathermen got excited; and since everybody is interested in the weather, it was not long before the second condition of progress was manifest: a felt need for international cooperation.

There remained the need for an international institution to put available technology to work in the common interest. This would complete the preconditions for agreement on the things that draw nations together.

In 1951—six years before the first Sputnik—the antique professional society called the International Meteorological Organization had become an intergovernmental agency with executive capacity called the World Meteorological Organization, affiliated with the United Nations as a Specialized Agency.

In 1961—four years after Sputnik I—President Kennedy laid down a challenge to the United Nations: to design a global weather reporting and forecasting system for the benefit of every nation in the world, a World Weather Watch, as it came to be called. With such a system it may become possible to provide reasonably accurate daily weather forecasts for periods of up to two weeks ahead, compared to a still primitive forecast for three days at the best today.

The implications are breath-taking—for agriculture, for flood control, for navigation, for tourism, for sports and recreation—for every nation with airplanes to fly, every firm with work to be done outdoors, every family planning a weekend outing or a wedding reception on the lawn.

The World Weather Watch will not be ready tomorrow, but the planning is moving ahead at the WMO and in the national weather bureaus, especially our own. There is plenty of engineering ahead, political and social engineering as well as the other kind. But we are on our way, and there is no reason to think we will not have a functioning global observation system by early in the seventies.

Somewhat further in the future lies the exciting prospect of purposeful modification of the weather by man—of minimizing the incidence and the severity of hurricanes, tornadoes, and other violent storms—of influencing the level of precipitation and perhaps modifying temperatures. This will depend upon basic research which is not yet done but is getting under way.

There is no sound basis at this time for predicting when we may acquire the awesome power to alter the climate upon which human and other life depends. But when the time comes, as almost surely it will, it is a power that cannot rest in the hands of any one nation. President Johnson said it when he sent to Congress a 1965 National Science Foundation Report on Weather Modification: ". . . it is clear that large-scale weather or climate control schemes cannot be contained within national boundaries."

We will not want other nations modifying our weather, and we will certainly have to accept restraints on our freedom to modify theirs.

The agreements that will make a global system of the world's weather envelope are just an illustration of the proposition that international politics is not a zero-sum game in which an inch gained by one player must mean an inch lost by another.

The reality is that international agreements can be reached, international organizations can be formed, and international common law can be elaborated on subjects which draw nations together even as they continue to quarrel about the frontiers and friends and ideological frenzies that keep them apart.

Let us look for a moment, then, at the political merits of functional organizations: the kind that work at peace through meteorology, or health, or food, or education and training, or communications, or culture, or postal service, or children, or money, or economic growth, or the exploration of outer space—organizations, that is, for the pursuit of some specific and definable task beyond the frontiers of one nation, a task for which the technology is already conceived or conceivable, for which a common interest is mutually recognized, for which institutions can—and therefore must—be designed.

• Organizations like these *begin by taking the world as it is.* No fundamental political reforms are needed; no value systems have to be altered; no ideologies have to be seriously compromised.

• These organizations *start from where we are, and then take the next step.* And that, as the ancient Chinese guessed long ago, is the only way to get from here to there.

• These organizations *tackle jobs that can be managed through imperfect institutions by fallible men and women.* Omniscience is not a prerequisite; the peace of the world does not stand or fall on the success of any one organization; mistakes need not be fatal.

• These limited-purpose organizations *bypass the obstacle of sovereignty.* National independence is not infringed when a nation voluntarily accepts in its own interest the restraints imposed by cooperation with others. Nobody has to play who does not want to play. But among those who do play, there are door prizes for all.

• These organizations built around an agreed task can readily *achieve a reasonable balance between power and representation in* the control of the organization. In the General Assembly of the United Nations, the principle of one vote for each nation is sacrosanct. But in a functional organization it is possible to work out ways in which those who contribute most of the resources can take a larger responsibility for decisions as to how those resources will be used. In the International Labor Organization, the industrial nations have a special position; in the International Maritime Consultative Organization, the big shipping nations, including Norway, have a special voice. In the U.N.'s Outer Space Committee, there is an unwritten rule that the nations actually engaged in exploring space will act by consensus rather than fail to act by taking votes. And in the United Nations Security Council, of course, the special right of veto is reserved to the great powers by the Charter itself.

• Finally, these task-oriented organizations *can readily grow with the need and adapt to the new tasks made possible by new technologies.* Healthy institutions, like healthy cells, grow organically, by evolution.

None of these advantages of the functional approach to world integration is theoretical. The International Postal Union survived two world wars that left the wreckage of political agreements scattered all over Europe. The League of Nations fell apart, but functional organizations—for weights and measures, narcotics control, labor standards, and the rest—all survived and are going stronger today than when Stalin, Hitler, Mussolini, and the Japanese militarists walked out of the League. The General Assembly of the United Nations was out of business for a year over a political-constitutional point, but during the same year the Specialized Agencies and affiliated organs working at functional tasks actually expanded the scale of their activity. And in the midst of turmoil in Southeast Asia, the Committee on the Lower Mekong Basin continues to work in routine and astonishing harmony.

The Caricature of Foreign Aid

8

We do not need new knowledge to make this planet a decent place to live. We have plenty of tested ideas now.

We know how to grow and preserve enough food to conquer hunger; and beyond that, we know how to multiply the yield of food from the seas. We know how to provide the average infant with a diet that gives him a chance to develop his physical and intellectual potential.

We know how to survey and conserve water resources, how to develop river basins for many purposes, how to irrigate land and build power plants and develop enough industry to make enough goods to meet the needs of even the swollen population of this earth. We know how the poorer countries can leapfrog some of the traditional stages of development. Now that we can transport solids by pipeline, some countries can avoid heavy investment in railroads. With electric power to bring industry to underemployed farmers, some countries will be able to avoid the social costs of building factories in big cities. With small investment in ground stations, they will be able to plug into the World Weather Watch. With communication satellites and television and computers as tools and new concepts of social science as stimulus, they can educate their children better than our grandfathers were educated. And with modern ways of finding out what is in the ground, they can get at their resources more quickly and more profitably than we did in our nation's youth.

Yet despite the hum of men and women at work on development projects in every country of the globe, the outlook mocks our present knowledge. Our poor triumphs fail to match our rich technology.

It is, for example, appalling—it is an intolerable statistic—that the diet of two out of three people on earth is more likely to deteriorate than to improve in the years just ahead. Can we do something about it? Can we, say, feed 6 billion people by the year 2000? Can we double total farm production and triple the output of milk, meat, eggs, and fish? On the record—the record of miraculous technology—we probably can.

If Ceylonese motorboats can multiply by ten the fish brought in with boats propelled by oar; if a general use of hybrid corn would double the world's supply of corn; if a dairy cow in one part of Asia can produce 25 times the milk of her counterpart in other parts of Asia; if the Japanese can produce more rice per square inch than anybody else; if only one acre of land is now cultivated for each person in the world and another two-and-one-half acres are probably tillable; if the world's most densely populated nation can earn foreign exchange as a net exporter of food; if in our own country one farmer can feed his own family and 26 others—then there is still plenty of room for the human race on this compacted globe, and the vision of a world free from hunger is a realistic goal and not a pipe dream.

They spoke of these matters at the Hot Springs Conference a generation ago, and one historian of the U.N. Charter summarized the outcome thus: "Its immediate results consist largely of fairly obvious generalizations and recommendations." It has long been "fairly obvious" that too many people are hungry. But a generation ago it was not so clear to so many that something could be done about it. Now the scandal is that we are not doing it, in food or in a dozen other fields that comprise the science and art of "development."

The story of our approach to an international war on poverty is the story of a series of fashions, each giving way to another conception of the one true "key to development." We are able now to see development as an inclusive and complex process, not as the automatic product of some selected stimulus. But it has been hard going. As technical conferences have opened and closed, as bilateral aid programs have come to grips with realities in the field, as the U.N. agencies reached out for practical things to do about development in individual countries, specialist enthusiasms first held sway.

One by one the advocates of one-shot solutions came forward and discovered a new key to economic growth and social progress in the world's poorer lands. Each expert enthusiasm left its mark on the developing doctrines of development. Each soon gave way to another as a focus of attention, yet retained some place in an evolving pattern of increasingly sophisticated action.

Relief and rehabilitation came first. World War II had destroyed so much that the first thought was to put things back together the way they had been. In Europe and China, the institutional expression of this drive was the U.N. Relief and Rehabilitation Administration. It spent nearly $3 billion, mostly on food and raw materials; it invented some of the workways that are still proving valuable, such as the concept that receiving countries should put up "counterpart funds" in their own currencies, matching the value of goods brought in from the outside. And UNRRA found there was a limit to what could be done from the outside, if the country being helped did not have the trained people and the domestic institutions to absorb the imported aid.

The China program of UNRRA tried to spend two-thirds of a billion dollars in a country that lacked transportation and trained people, and was in the midst of a civil war and a raging monetary inflation. It was just too much; when I arrived in Shanghai to manage UNRRA's China Office in 1947, I found evidences of indigestion all over the docks of that crowded port—especially, wheat and flour moldering in godowns because there was no way to get it to the workers on development projects a thousand miles inland. When scholars later theorized about the limits of "absorptive capacity" for aid, I thought I had perhaps been witness to the clearest case in which the outsiders had tried to do too much too fast with too little cooperation from the insiders.

When the Chinese Nationalists were pushed off the mainland and began to govern from the island of Formosa, the lessons which government leaders and American aiders had learned were put to good use; massive aid was more carefully planned; new kinds of institutions were built, such as the famous Joint Commission on Rural Reconstruction, which sponsored land reform along with efforts to increase rice productivity. Formosa in time became a showplace of successful foreign aid, and eventually led the list of countries which "graduated" from U.S. aid to economic self-support.

The second enthusiasm—*recovery by outside investment*—worked in Europe and was carried over into the thinking about Asia, Africa, and Latin America, with results that slowed down sensible thinking about the development of the poor countries.

It worked in Europe because the problem was essentially to rebuild, with more modern machinery, the kinds of economies that the war had destroyed. This effort was phenomenally successful; yet even in Europe it left big pockets of poverty, in Greece, southern Italy, and elsewhere, inadequately attended to, and failed to equalize opportunity for the children of lower classes of societies still characterized by an economic caste system.

In the poorer continents, the formula would not work, and the thinking of people responsible for aid programs turned to deeper involvement in those "internal affairs" that were clearly the limiting factors to effective outside support of programs for economic growth.

Thus *technical assistance,* as the deep involvement of outsiders came to be called, became the next fashion. This fitted our own American feeling, the product of our national experience, that no problem is insoluble if enough of the right kinds of technical experts are turned loose to solve it. Development is people, the lecturers would say in the overseas training courses. And applicants for a role in the aid program would generally say they wanted to work abroad because they liked to work with people. In the fifties, Congressional presentations on foreign aid began to soft-pedal the balance of payments statistics and to introduce instead a county agent from Kentucky who would explain in a bucolic accent how a handful of broom corn and a good technical man had resulted in a whole new broom industry for the Shan States of Burma. This kind of testimony was enormously popular on Capitol Hill for a time; so popular with some legislators that they would approve the technical aid parts of the foreign aid program, which were comparatively inexpensive, and justify their votes to cut investment aid with speeches pointing out that development is basically a matter of people and skills, not money.

The problems which American and other technicians solved in the poor countries were indeed impressive. Great roads were built, great health hazards eliminated, great rivers harnessed, great ports expanded. But the results were happenstance. Where an effective outsider was teamed with an effective official or technician within the developing country, remarkable tasks were accomplished. But often the outsider was clumsy or the insider inept, or both, and the resulting development effort reflected more the accidents of personality than the priorities of need.

Development planning then came to be the watchword. Money and technical aid should be given only to those countries which put together a first-rate development plan and presented it to assure the outsiders that the outside help would be properly fitted to a rational sense of what internal resources were available, and for what purpose they would be used. This surge projected into the lives of the poor countries a large number of very bright economists and other thoughtful folk, most of them from countries (like the United States) which would not touch central economic planning at home, but who threw themselves with enthusiasm and modern mathematics into the task of planning the economies of large and small nations in other continents.

It was a notable step forward—not because "planning" was the panacea that some of the planners supposed, but because it enabled the central managers and top political leaders of many countries to develop a way of thinking about their own priorities, and to begin to govern and control the strong alliances that had already sprung up between inside specialists and outside specialists in each of the major fields of development: health, agriculture, industry, transportation, banking, and the like.

The planners soon discovered that the real bottleneck to rapid economic growth was the absence of enough trained people, especially in those ex-colonial countries where most of the managerial functions had traditionally been performed by outsiders. So *training institutes* and elaborate plans for educating Asians and Africans and Latin Americans in Europe and the United States came to be the vogue. The result has been a truly enormous increase in the stockpile of technical skills—not always accompanied by equally impressive political judgments by the "been-tos," the students who have been to Paris or London or any one of dozens of American universities.

Curiously, one of the results of this mass production of technicians was to reveal our inability to train people who could build institutions and run them; they often learned from their European or American technical advisers how to advise, but not how to take the operating responsibility themselves. Moreover, the kinds of planners who were being trained by the economics departments of leading graduate schools were good at conceiving sensible and balanced goals for development, but often not very good at figuring out what was supposed to happen after the Prime Minister had signed The Plan.

This led to the discovery of *institution building* as the key to development, and a growing emphasis on training whole teams of people who could take over a Ministry of Finance or build a rural credit bank or manage a hospital or medical school. Technical assistance in *public administration* became the rage. And then the paradox of exporting ideas and talent was nakedly revealed: We are, it seems, better at exporting what we don't have than at teaching others how we accomplish what we do. We teach central economic planning with more enthusiasm and fewer uncertainties than public administration, and this is strange because the genius of American society is precisely our capacity to build and manage large, complex administrative structures without elaborate advance planning. Whatever the reason, our technical aid in public administration was too often conceived as just another specialty, rather than as training for leadership in an environment of rapid change, which is to say a political environment.

Somewhere along the line, the more thoughtful participants in the aid business began to wonder whether economic growth was an adequate target for an economic development program. Expanding Gross National Product seemed to be combined, in too many parts of the "developing world," with urban misery and falling per capita incomes.

One result of this rethinking was more talk about *social development*. For a while this meant that experts on social welfare should be somehow related to the aid programs; there was even an abortive attempt to add "social welfare attachés" to a number of American embassies abroad. But success in applying social work techniques to pockets of urban poverty in the United States did not seem to be highly transferable when the problem was the poverty of the whole rural societies. The *"community development"* concept, adapted from Jimmy Yen's Mass Education Movement and other pioneering efforts by missionary groups, did prove an important idea; thus another fashion was born. The idea was to concentrate on working at the village level, helping develop the leadership and the techniques locally for a coordinated attack on illiteracy, inefficiency in farming, debilitating diseases, insanitary water supplies, bad housing, and corrupt local government by a few educated overlords.

Much that is useful has been done along this line, notably in India. But the trouble is that the newly awakened people of Asia, Africa, and Latin America do not want to stay in their villages even if they are cleaned up. Students who go off to agricultural schools do not want to go back to live with their parents and try to persuade them to modernize; they want to find a modern agricultural setup, or alternatively apply their new intellectual skills in the big city.

Banditry and boredom in the countryside, and bright lights and hoped-for job opportunities in the cities, have produced in every country a common experience—far too many people coming off the land and settling in the slum fringes around the main cities. They are economically miserable, but often no more so than they were in the village; and at least they have plenty of company, and the chance to demonstrate in the streets for or against whatever political leaders they are paid or persuaded to favor or oppose. This is why, in the first ten years after independence, Indonesia's capital of Djakarta grew from a sleepy colonial capital of 300,000 to a vibrant and volatile national capital of 3 million persons; other cities in the developing nations have grown in proportion, and with as little justification in trade or industry.

In the first twenty years of postwar development, urban population has everywhere grown much faster than urban jobs. The answer to this universal state of affairs is not merely social relief programs in the urban fringes, though these are now more necessary than ever. The answer is certainly not to try to persuade people to go back to their villages, or stay there if they have not yet moved into town; as Margaret Mead says, we have for too long been trying to stockpile the surplus population in rural areas abroad the way we store surplus agricultural commodities in rural areas at home. Probably the answer lies in the direction the regional planners now seem to favor: the development of intermediate towns, with more job opportunities than the cities can create and more attractions for educated people than are or can be available at the village level.

The perception that more production has not always meant less misery focuses attention on the growth of *population*. Death control has been proceeding apace, through broad and remarkably successful programs aimed at the main diseases that kill people in the developing countries, malaria and malnourishment and schistosomiasis and yaws, rather than the heart diseases and cancer that cause death in the more developed nations where people live longer. Birth control, though, is still a primitive technique and a sensitive topic.

On the whole, the efforts of the demographers to scare the world with grotesque "estimates" of the world's future population are not very helpful in getting the subject down to earth. But there is good news these days on the population front—the "population explosion" has become a respectable subject. Both President Kennedy and President Johnson have helped lift the taboo from public discussion of one of the prime topics of public policy in our time.

A few years ago it was considered politically impossible to inscribe the subject of population control on a U.N. agenda for rational debate. But in 1963 the General Assembly passed an eminently sensible resolution on the subject which offended nobody yet opened the way for much-needed research and for further U.N. work on the subject.

In that process everyone discovered, to the surprise of most, that the only disagreement is on the outside fringes of a very large subject, and there is a wide area of common ground on which intelligent men from every culture and every religious tradition can converge for dispassionate discourse and cooperative action.

No one can hazard even an educated guess as to when or how the population growth rate may be brought within manageable limits. Birth rates in industrialized countries have eventually, though slowly, declined without much encouragement from governments. Now several countries, notably Japan, India, Pakistan, Korea, and the united Arab republic, are launched on active government programs to reduce explosive population growth rates. But by and large, when it comes to population control there are no developed and underdeveloped countries.

Unlike agriculture or industry or public health or almost any other subject, there is no place to go to learn how somebody else did it first. In the population field, international technical assistance starts from scratch, with little national experience to go on. That is all the more reason for serious professional attention to the matter. And one technical fact at least is reasonably clear: the "plastic coil" for the first time makes it economically feasible for whole populations, however poor, to avoid having so many children that they offset everything else that is done in the field of economic and social development.

The way is clear now for serious discussion and vigorous international action to control a trend which, if uncontrolled, would commit the search for freedom from hunger to a perpetual treadmill or a chronic failure.

Two "fashions" remain to be discovered before the spectrum of development is seen whole. It is clear that poor *internal security* is a mighty contributor to poverty in many developing nations. The U.S. aid program has included some police training and a good deal of military aid. Yet a comprehensive concept of development would of course have to include both the development of military forces and the development of the economy.

The other missing factor is some way for outsiders to help in the development of *political organizations*. This is the most sensitive subject of all, of course, for the most obvious form of "intervention in the internal affairs" of another country is to help some group of political leaders organize their struggle for political power. Yet it is the absence of effective political organization that causes instability which makes it hard to carry through programs of economic and social development.

The reluctance to touch military and political development, and the tendency to separate them from the economic and social programs, was well illustrated by the United Nations' performance in the Congo. The unnoticed success of the U.N.'s civil programs should somehow be celebrated—U.N. technicians brought together from all over the world (and from every international specialized agency) managed the airports, cleaned up the water supply, provided nearly all the medical care, staffed most of the schools with teachers, rebuilt the internal transportation system, tamped down a dangerous inflation, suppressed much of the smuggling, re-established trade, and encouraged the return of outside investment.

If there is a government that governs at all in the Congo, it is because that government was put in business, and its functionaries trained, by U.N. (and also by the remaining Belgian) technicians, while the U.N. peace-keeping force was taking care of three armed secessions—one led by communists in the north, one led by diamond smugglers in a central province, and one based on copper revenues in Katanga.

Yet, looking back on the U.N. operation in the Congo, it is clear that the absence of two factors from the United Nations' mandate led to some of the major troubles which beset the Congo after the U.N. peace-keeping force departed in mid-1964. One missing link was the training of the Congolese National Army, which the U.N. force did not think it had the authority to do; the other was the development of a national political party, or more than one, which could begin to organize Congolese loyalties around concepts and leaders rather than around ancient tribal affiliations that are increasingly irrelevant to the making of a modern society in that potentially rich and prosperous land.

As one fashion gave way to another, and that to yet another, people concerned with economic and social development began to mute their doctrinaire claims that the key to development everywhere was to be found in anyone's pet theory or favorite dogma. The hope for a sudden blinding flash of clarity, the illusion of a single solution, a simple answer, or a secret formula, has faded in the clash of ideas and the commerce of shared experience that have informed our thinking.

I am not saying that relief, recovery, investment, technical assistance, planning, education and training, institution building, public administration, community development, population control, internal security, and political development are not important or crucial. Indeed, I would cheerfully concede that they are *all* "keys to development." Advocacy, even strident advocacy, of one or another of these factors has served sometimes to bring it into clearer focus and better balance with the other major factors in economic and social development. They are all more or less important at various stages of growth, and various times and places. The point is that they are intimately and intricately interrelated. Most societies have to work on most of them most of the time. But the best mix of them, the best formula for applying all the perceptions and tools and kinds of specialists in one country, is highly unlikely to be the best formula for another country. In development as in peace-keeping the goal is freedom—which is to say a workable diversity, not an overworked dogma.

We are still working to perceive the process of economic and social growth clearly; but at least we see it as a process, and we are beginning to see it whole.

Against the background of so complex a task, it is small wonder that people who read only the more sensationalized accounts in the annual Congressional debate should come to feel that development assistance is a hapless, hopeless chore. The overdrawn press stories produce, it seems to me, a badly distorted caricature, compounded of five illusions:

First, that the very process of economic and social growth—what starts it, what keeps it going, how an outsider can best help—is an unfathomable mystery.

Second, that the task of helping other countries is a lonely burden, borne quite unfairly by long-suffering Uncle Sam.

Third, that foreign aid is an endless task at a growing cost to the American taxpayer.

Fourth, that the Communists do this sort of thing better than we do.

Fifth, that there is no real support in our domestic politics for foreign aid.

These impressions, all of them, are false. Let us examine them with the fishy eye they deserve.

Certainly we do not yet know all we need to know about the subject. What, for example, is the role of political leadership in creating a national "will to grow"? How does one go about rooting out corruption in societies where it has become part of the national fabric? How and at what pace can one change, without producing social trauma, customs which frustrate growth? There are many tough questions like these; and to all of them must be added the even tougher question: How, in each country, can outsiders help the insiders build their own free institutions without making things worse?

I sometimes think that stimulating and managing the modernization process is the most complex and delicate task of social engineering ever consciously undertaken by man. It is full of pitfalls, and those who are working at it will surely tumble into some of them. But as our own pioneers learned on the American prairie, it is no good to have the courage to begin without the strength to continue.

We have not been long at this task, but we have learned much—from mistakes, needless to say. One mistake, which can also be seen as a necessary part of our education, was to swing wildly from one to another of the specialist nostrums to which I have already referred. Another mistake was to set out breezily to transfer wholesale the institutions and ideas of the economically dynamic to the static societies. And when it transpired that we could not dig a hole and plant there a replica of some European or American institution, many Europeans and Americans suffered a sentimental revulsion and swung the other way: The developed countries, we were told, should concentrate on doing for the less developed what the "people themselves" wanted done.

But there were problems about carrying this idea into action, too. Who were "the people," in countries where elections were either rigged or absent? It is not easy to analyze the rapid mutation of political power in somebody else's country. Another difficulty was that the leaders of the developing countries tended to make the same mistake we had earlier made: that is, they thought that what *they* wanted was what *we* already had.

So we are indeed only beginning to learn how to make a creative blend of *our* technology and administrative skills and *their* folkways and workways—building modern-style institutions out of local cultural raw materials. The state of our theory about how to do this, how to transfer and adapt the growth inducing elements from one society to another, is still woefully short of the practitioners' needs. But we know incomparably more than we did twenty years ago.

We know that a few miles of road in the wilderness, an isolated health center, a country schoolhouse, a clean-up campaign in one village do not add up to a development process. We know that it is much harder, and takes longer, to grow people than to grow anything else. We know that the most useful measuring rods in development are those which measure the building and competent use of modern institutions (from ministries and whole cities to schools and experiment stations), rather than those which measure only production, national income, or the balance of trade and payments. We know that the vigorous effort by most technical specialists to exclude politics and internal security factors from their calculations is doomed to failure. We know that technicians who leave going institutions behind are good technicians, and technicians who just leave techniques behind are bad technicians—even if everybody loves them and they are fairly dripping with cultural empathy.

These are important lessons, even if they indicate more clearly what not to do than just how to proceed. If we cannot yet provide pat answers, we can at least define the questions in all their fascinating complexity. It is quite a lot to learn in twenty years. If we apply in the next twenty years what we have already learned since the war, the foreign aid program is almost bound to be a success—measured by the number, variety, and quality of free institutions other peoples will have created with our help.

The second component of our caricature is that the United States is carrying the whole load of helping others to modernize their institutions. It is true that we were the first in the field. It is also true that the burden sharing is still somewhat uneven. But during these twenty years, a growing proportion of all "foreign aid" has been provided by other countries, and by international agencies in which we pay only 30 or 40 per cent of the cost. There are economic aid agencies now in London, Paris, Bonn, and Tokyo, and in Rome, Brussels, Bern, The Hague, Tel Aviv, Stockholm, Copenhagen and a couple of dozen other places as well. According to the definition of "foreign aid" adopted by the Organization for Economic Cooperation and Development, which compares aid with per capita Gross National Product, the United States' aid program is proportionately not the largest but the fifth largest in the world today.

We work through more than two dozen international organizations which are in the "foreign aid" business, including the World

Bank, the International Development Association, the International Finance Corporation, and the nine Specialized Agencies of the United Nations, which in turn get their aid money mostly through the U.N. Special Fund and the Expanded Program of Technical Assistance. The U.N. family of organizations is now the world's largest source of assistance to developing countries, with the sole and probably temporary exception of our own bilateral aid program. We are typically the largest stockholder in these enterprises, as we should be and want to be. But hundreds of millions of dollars are put in by other countries, totaling far more than we contribute. Indeed, one of the good things about working at economic development through international agencies is that it helps make sure that others are doing their part.

Thus, we are certainly not in this thing by ourselves. Only if we were out of it, would we be all alone.

This proliferation of effort, spurred in part by the American insistence that others chip in too, is not necessarily all to the good. The Communists have joined the game, stressing political influence rather than economic growth. And even apart from the Communists, the internationalization of aid has enormously increased the complexity of an already complicated task.

Between twenty and thirty outside organizations are now purveying technical assistance and development loans in the typical developing country. The multiplication of outsiders leads of course to competition and overlapping; it places on the receiving country the obligation to coordinate all these outsiders, which burdens underdeveloped countries at just the point where they are usually the most underdeveloped, that is to say, in their ability to coordinate complex operations. But it does increase the resources available for development, and for the more sophisticated of the developing nations it provides a golden opportunity to play the assorted agencies and bilateral programs off against each other for economic advantage and political protection.

We used to assure ourselves that the old argument about bilateral aid versus multilateral aid was obsolete and buried. Obviously, both are needed and have been needed for twenty years, and will doubtless be needed for decades more.

But this hardy little pest, like the anopheles mosquito, turns out to be more durable than we thought, and his earlier death was perhaps exaggerated. It used to be that people who were enthusiastic about bilateral aid tried to prove we ought to do as much as possible bilaterally in order to get credit for the generosity of the U.S. taxpayer. Now there seem to be a good many people who think it all ought to be done by multilateral means, mostly because they are disenchanted with the amount of political credit which aid programs can garner in foreign countries.

The policy of the United States is clear on this. We want to do, and are trying to do, as much as possible of the aid job through international channels. There are some obvious advantages to doing this: International agencies can draw on a worldwide pool of technical people, they can sponsor regional projects that cut across national frontiers, and they typically cost us 40 cents or less on the dollar, which is certainly better than financing the whole process ourselves.

But this policy of ours—to do as much as possible through international agencies—is much less openhanded than it sounds. There are stringent limitations on what and how much can be done through international organizations. These limitations mean that only a fraction of the total development assistance required can realistically be administered internationally.

A prime limitation is that international organizations are even harder to administer efficiently than are national organizations operating in international agencies. The budgets of the United Nations and its Specialized Agencies have been going up much faster than the budgets of most of the contributing countries in recent years; the average rate of increase for the U.N. Specialized Agencies has been in the neighborhood of 15 per cent per year. This has been an enormous strain on the administrative capacity of some of the agencies to do the tasks the nations have assigned to them. UNESCO is overstrained in this respect today, and several of the other agencies are also straining at the seams.

The United States will no doubt continue to press for growth of international development agencies, and of other contributors' bilateral programs. But it is essential that they grow at a reasonable pace and in an orderly way. Otherwise, they will trample each other's feet so much that they will ruin hard-won reputations for effective action in many fields over the past twenty years. We will have to work hard to make sure that they work together, as they grow.

The third component of the foreign aid caricature is the impression that the need for aid is a bottomless pit, that the development road runs through a long curving tunnel with no light at the end, that the cost of economic growth and social progress is beyond measure and the task is without limit.

Worldwide development is indeed expensive, and we cannot today put a price tag on the job of setting the whole world on the road to self-sustaining growth. But that is not because the cost is so astronomical as to be immeasurable; it is simply that we do not yet know enough to measure it with any real accuracy.

Of course, this will be a long-term job. And unfortunately we cannot today establish a terminal date for aid, as we were able to do with the Marshall Plan. But we do know that it will be shorter if we think of it as long range. There will come a peak, after which the load of external "aid" will begin to taper off.

Already some major clients of our foreign aid program—most of the countries in Europe, plus Japan—have shifted over from net recipients to net contributors in international development. Greece and Formosa are recently off the economic aid list, and half a dozen more countries may soon be strong enough to follow their example. As to the remainder, some 100 "developing" countries and territories, it is important to keep in mind that most of the problem is concentrated in a relatively few large societies which are already in the category of the "semi-developed."

Forty per cent of the total population of the "developing world" —Asia, Africa, and Latin America—lives in just two countries. Is it beyond the realm of reason that India and Brazil could, with maximum efforts now, reach a stage of growth during this Decade of Development where massive inputs of government-to-government aid no longer will be required? Or, to put it another way: India and Pakistan, sharing a single subcontinent, have more people than all of Latin America and Africa put together. Some 40 per cent of our economic aid has been going to those two countries. Is it beyond reason that they could, in a decade of hard work and mutual peace, be earning a considerably larger share of their own way toward self-sustaining growth?

In the meantime, there is a limit to the levels of external assistance, especially capital assistance, which can be absorbed effectively by the developing institutions in the developing countries. We do not know just what the global level is, but probably it is not very much higher than the present rate of flow. So the demand is not unlimited, whatever that limit is. Moreover, the aid-exporting nations will be sharing the so-called burden on, we hope, an increasingly equitable basis. And as the leading countries now in the "less developed" category move toward modernization, they too can begin to share in the common enterprise, as Chile, India, Israel, Egypt, and others are already beginning to do.

We should certainly work harder at the job of establishing at least tentative target dates for self-sustaining growth and of estimating the price tag for reasonably well defined stages. But whether or not we can do this with any degree of accuracy in the period immediately ahead, the task is finite in cost and finite in duration.

The fourth face of the caricature is that the Communists are better at the foreign aid business than we are.

An interesting study could be made of their mistakes compared to ours. My own observation is that they have learned remarkably little from watching us. They started by making their foreign aid program a slavish copy of ours. Then they proceeded systematically to make the same mistakes we made, in the same order in which we made them, with an average lag of four to five years.

They built large concrete "monuments," and put bronze plaques on them, and found that the gratitude for large visible projects like sports stadiums and office buildings hardly lasts as long as it takes to complete the construction job. They sent "ugly Russians" to live in haughty compounds. They brought African students to Moscow and treated them as second-class citizens. They even thought for a time—as a dwindling number of Americans still do—that aid was the road to popularity.

They made technical errors. The Soviet engineers who were sent cement made for dry climates watched in despair as it hardened in the humidity of the port of Rangoon. Another group of Soviet aid officials must have had a similar sinking feeling when they saw the arrival of fur clothing for use in Guinea, which is on the Equator with temperatures to match; or when they saw construction equipment built for use in Siberia melt and fuse in 120° tropical heat; or when a fine Soviet radio station given to an African country failed to work because Soviet technicians had built it right on top of a vein of iron.

Above all, they overplayed their political hand—in the Middle East, then in Africa, then in Cuba. They reached into the developing countries to grasp the levers of power, not realizing that those levers first had to be created before anybody could manipulate them, for good or ill. The Communists have not been able to hide their ambition to make every nation beholden to one doctrine and one totalitarian system of power. And that is an insuperable handicap in a world peopled by men and women with a growing capacity to tell the difference between outsiders who want them to be free and outsiders who want to see them enslaved.

The final illusion in the foreign aid caricature is that nobody in the United States really likes it.

In American politics the economic progress and social problems of the "developing" countries—which means all of Asia, Africa, and Latin America—are associated with the annual spasm of our own foreign aid legislation. The money bill for foreign aid usually has the distinction of being the last reluctant act of each expiring Congress; in the second month of Lyndon Johnson's Presidency, Congressmen were called back for an extraordinary early morning session on Christmas Eve to pass a foreign aid bill before joining their families for what was left of the holiday season.

The popularity of pessimism is nowhere more in evidence than in debates about foreign aid. In Congress and out, foreign aid seems to attract the gloomiest attention of those professional star-gazers, entrails sorters, numerologists, demographers, and economists who make their reputations by predicting that problems faced by the United States of America are too big or too difficult for Americans to tackle. The net impression from their jeremiads, featuring as they do American blunders, cutbacks, retreats, punched pillows, rat holes, deadbeats, and dead ends, is that the task of overseas development is hopeless and the program an uncharted swamp.

The management of foreign aid is no bed of roses—unless you count the thorns. It is immensely complex, enormously difficult, and not a little frustrating. It requires the deepest kind of involvement in the internal affairs of other countries—which means that successes are always to the credit of the government of the developing country, while failures are naturally blamed on the outsiders.

Economic and social development has as many facets as human society, and foreign aid, as part of it, is a many-purpose tool. Maybe this is why the purposes and limitations of foreign aid are so little understood.

Economic aid is like water coming from a hose. The water can be used for many purposes: to put out leaf fires, to wash the car, to cool off the children in summer, to break up a dog fight, or even to water the lawn. To ask, "Is the water successful?" is to ask another preconditioning question, "What was it being used for?"

Thus, aid is used to relieve victims of disaster, to get a strategic base, to help allies build their armed strength, to stave off economic collapse. It is used to promote international development, that is, to help build free institutions inside other people's countries and help the people there to make those free institutions work. We should not be disappointed if aid given to build a military highway fails to raise more rice or reduce the death rate from malaria. We should be disappointed only if aid designed to build free institutions fails to build free institutions.

Most Americans do not thus ration their disappointments about what foreigners do with our aid, and it is widely regarded as good politics to be vaguely against the foreign aid program. That program will remain under attack—it is only later that it will be judged with a more compassionate and discerning eye. Those of us who worked in the European Recovery Program vividly recall that when the Marshall Plan was first proposed, loud voices were raised to proclaim that it would bankrupt the United States, build Socialism in Europe, and merely add to the strength of Europe when the Communists swallowed it all up. We also remember that when it became clear that the Marshall Plan was a brilliant success, the critics were suddenly for it, and a remarkable number of people revealed that they had suggested it first. "Ten cities vied for Homer dead, where Homer living begged his bread."

In the annual debate, the supporters of foreign aid stress the economics of the poor countries, while the opponents of aid talk mostly about the politics of the poor countries. Cutting off economic aid is the standard remedy suggested for loose-lipped talk by foreign political leaders and anti-American demonstrations by their supporters. Our deep involvement in their affairs through economic (and sometimes military) aid is of course a major issue in the domestic politics of each recipient nation. The opposition typically campaigns against American intervention (it always is safer to attribute your nation's troubles to outsiders) so the government often feels it has to do some of the same, to take the political wind out of the opposition's sails. And just as most foreigners know little of American politics, and tend to assume that any Senator speaks for the United States, so Americans fail to see anti-American statements by foreign politicians as ploys in domestic political rivalries.

In spite of these obstacles to universal popularity, the U.S. foreign aid program has never lacked the support of Presidents and the consent of Congress. The standard annual cut ranging from 10 to 15 per cent that once seemed accepted without excitement by the recipient nations has given way to the "bikini budget." Public opinion polls on U.S. attitudes toward foreign aid generally turn up around 60 per cent for and 30 per cent against. But the most interesting thing revealed by these polls is *why* people favor foreign aid.

Had they been listening to official Washington all these years, the American people would favor foreign aid, if at all, for hardheaded reasons of national interest, narrowly conceived—because it helps frustrate the Communists (which it does), and because it is good for American business and American farmers (which it is). But when the professional probers probe for the reasons behind a favorable feeling toward foreign aid, people reply with sentiments heard more often in churches than in Congressional hearings: ". . . because it's our duty to help other people less fortunate than ourselves."

This sense of obligation, so deeply felt by so many yet so seldom articulated in official justifications, is I think the real political underpinning that gives continuity to U.S. aid contributions that reach into every non-Communist society on the face of the earth. This, more than any other reason, explains why every year the leaders of an impressive cross section of the major private membership organizations in this country parade to Capitol Hill to testify in support of one or another segment of a bipartisan foreign aid bill. And this is why every President and every Presidential candidate since World War II has come out publicly and repeatedly for continuing aid to the economies of the developing nations.

To match the depth and breadth of this support, we need a governmental commitment to a program large enough in resources and long enough in duration to match the problem itself.

It is good that the world's rich are getting richer—and fast. But it is bad that despite our considerable efforts most of the world's poor are still getting poorer—absolutely in some cases, relatively in most. In some other century this state of affairs might have been the occasion for leisurely scholarship and gentle tut-tutting in the drawing rooms of the rich. But in the 1960s and 1970s, the poor are mobilized into nations, as we wanted them to be, and will insist on rather more than a fair shake from the rest of us. If they do not get it, we might as well shelve any plans to build a "workable world order" for as far ahead as we can see.

It is time we admit to ourselves that the job is too big for half measures, and too urgent for "emergency" aid. We are still making the costly mistake of tackling twenty-year problems with five-year plans using two-year personnel working with one-year appropriations. It is not good enough.

Peace and
Human Rights

9

From 100 miles up, the earth looks blue and beautiful—
and open—but on the ground the available land is carved up into
nations. Some are less beautiful than others, and many are not
open at all.

In a bare two decades, a billion people have been freed from
foreign rule and given their chance to build decent modern societies; only slightly more than 1 per cent of the world's people
remain in dependencies.

If you listen closely you can hear suggestive noises from the societies still closed. Listen to the poets and painters, to the philoso-
phers and composers, to the low drumbeat of doubts and the
muffled cross fire of questions, to the crackling creativity of the
open mind which no force on earth seems able to enslave for long.
For there is no dogma that can be transmitted through the genes.
No child is born an orthodox believer; he has to be carefully

taught. So every woman who gives birth in a closed society produces another threat to tyranny.

Nevertheless, human rights are suppressed as a matter of principle by political authorities controlling one-third of humanity; and most other authorities, including our own, have preferred to pursue human rights through national action. The underdeveloped area of international relations is the field of human rights. What can we do to make human rights operational in a world of a hundred sovereignties and several hundred thousand political jurisdictions?

In the U.N. Charter, the philosophical connection between peace and human rights was rather tenuous. Rights and peace were both there among the purposes, but the machinery had to do with how the nations would deal with each other, not how individual persons would deal with each other or how political authorities would treat their own people. This doctrinal circuit was closed by two declarations in the late spring of 1963. One was the last encyclical of Pope John XXIII, *Pacem in Terris,* which laid directly on political authorities the obligation to act by that simple but still revolutionary precept, "All men are equal in their natural dignity." The other was President Kennedy's commencement address at American University, in which by coincidence or design he made the same connection. "Is not peace," he asked, "basically a matter of human rights?" The members of the United Nations are not yet acting as if it were.

The Charter includes noble words on three subjects. In the United Nations' short history, the golden Charter words have been invoked against some twenty armed conflicts and at least twenty more near-wars. On thirteen occasions, as we have seen, they have provided the basis for the raising of a U.N. peace-keeping force.

In this same brief period, the Charter goal of "better standards of life in larger freedom" has served as inspiration for the beginnings of a worldwide war on poverty, prosecuted through a dozen specialized and affiliated agencies, spending and lending nearly $2 billion a year in 127 countries and territories.

But these same twenty years have produced little operational activity to match the explicit obligations of members to treat their own citizens as human beings should be treated. The question is: Do we want the United Nations, in the words to which we have all agreed in Article 55, to promote the "universal respect for, and observance of, human rights and fundamental freedoms for all without distinction as to race, sex, language or religion"? And do we seriously intend to take, as Article 56 enjoins us to take, "joint and separate action in cooperation with the Organization for the achievement of the purposes set forth in Article 55"?

The problem is, of course, that human rights and fundamental freedoms are mostly the product of decisions inside countries; and inside each country these decisions are the politically touchiest decisions of all.

Thus, the leaders of most nations were perfectly clear that they wanted a United Nations to protect the achievement of nationhood by pressing for the self-determination of peoples. But there is a good deal of uncertainty as to how far we and our fellow members want the U.N. to go in criticizing and correcting the ethical delinquencies of governments, once they have declared their national independence.

Since "human rights" have seemed so clearly within the boundaries of domestic jurisdiction, no country has been in the position to cast the first stone at the delinquencies of others. Each society (to stick with the Biblical imagery) has a plentiful supply of beams in its own eye. But in the United States we have at least moved out of the area of government-sponsored racial discrimination, and out of that second stage called "separate but equal," and into a brighter era for which a durable name has yet to be coined.

Because we are working hard on our own human rights problems, we need feel no embarrassment in asking whether every other government member of the United Nations is also working hard to promote human rights and fundamental freedoms for all within its own borders.

In the last two decades more than fifty new nations have sprung into being. By their enthusiasm for national independence they have focused the light of world opinion, and the machinery of the United Nations, on the remaining beachheads of empire. But national independence is only a first step to man's freedom—and not the most difficult step. The next steps have to do with self-government inside the nation. And inside each nation, as we have been rediscovering here at home, equal rights are but a hunting license for equal treatment.

Every people represented in the U.N. General Assembly has achieved freedom in the limited sense of separate nationhood. But how many of the governments there represented can in fairness and justice be said to have moved beyond *Plessy v. Ferguson,* beyond the "separate but equal" phase of the struggle for freedom?

This word "self-determination," which we use so often in U.N. resolutions and try to carry out in U.N. actions, was popularized by Woodrow Wilson to describe a process by which national boundaries would be wrapped around ethnic groups.

Because self-determination was often a racial battle cry, and the basis for nationalist revolutions, the resulting nations often had a racial foundation. Indeed, if you look around the world, or around the hall in the General Assembly, you can hardly avoid the conclusion that most of the world's nations, the newer ones and the older ones, have their foundations in some degree of racial separateness, and their government in the hands of one dominant racial group.

Too often in the modern nationalist revolution—let us say it with all honesty—the promise of freedom has been the promise of separateness.

In the fifty years just past, the shackles of contrived, legalized, enforced inequality have been—and rightly so—the chief devil in international relations. In Japan and along the China and India coasts, the shackles took the form of extraterritorial concessions; from Indonesia to West Africa, the shackles appeared as colonial governors and colonial troops and the serfdom of plantation economics; in Latin America, the shackles were oppressive land systems and labor practices.

For reasons of history, then, the clear and present devil in the nationalist revolution has generally been a foreign power, or foreign interest, or both, and the devil has generally been painted racially white. But now that almost all the world's peoples have achieved nationhood, we the peoples of the United Nations need to rethink these obsolete forms of deviltry.

The natural dignity of individual men and women and children is not threatened today in more than a handful of places by colonialists, which is to say, by foreigners. It is mostly threatened by the abuse of power by majorities—by the inhumanity of public man to private man.

The inhumanity of man to nearby man is of course an incident in the internal politics of nations, the continuation of the struggle for freedom inside a national society after nationhood has been achieved. Surely our dedication to freedom for "all Men" does not permit us to be unconcerned about inhumanity just because the men who practice it and their victims happen to be enclosed in a common national boundary. We may well be powerless to do anything effective about it, but we always have the power to care, and to complain out loud.

We hold, do we not, that the aspirations of equality and freedom for individual human beings—the achievement of the human dignity which is the natural right of every person—is not fulfilled:

• As long as governments manage their immigration to support racial discrimination;

• as long as governments do not allow persons of every race and religion to be citizens—and citizens of every race and religion to vote on a basis of equality;

• as long as governments do not treat every person as equal before the law;

• as long as governments do not allow non-members of the dominant racial group to seek political power.

If we still hold truths like these to be self-evident, then we have our work cut out for us. The winds of the sixties, the post-nationalist winds of freedom and equality for individuals, are blowing through every society represented in the United Nations, and through those that are not represented there, too. In political terms, every government in the world is threatened to some extent by these winds of the sixties. For most national leaders are not yet sure that it pays for everyone to be equal. There is no government in the world that fails to give lip service to the dignity of the human person, and there is no government that is doing everything it could do to protect and promote the Rights of Man.

There are and must be limits to the *international* concern with what each government, clothed with juridical sovereignty and the police power, is doing for and to the people over whom it has life and death control.

Virtually the whole world is enraged by South Africa's policy of *apartheid,* which is government-sponsored racial discrimination. Lacking any relevant human rights procedures in the United Nations, the new African nations have tried hard to stuff this human rights issue into the peace and security provisions of the Charter. They raise it periodically under this heading in the Security Council, and every autumn in the General Assembly. Resolutions are passed, but nothing happens, and the practice of *apartheid* goes on. Equally the repression of subject peoples, still so permanent and so repugnant a feature of Soviet policy and practice, is no less an issue of human rights for lack of a court in which the oppressed can complain of their oppression.

These are the standard instances. But we are also entitled to worry when we see (for example in Africa or the Middle East) racial bars to employment, racial bars to travel, and racial bars to citizenship; in one African country a white man cannot constitutionally become a citizen. Nearly every country has some forms of discriminatory trade and business arrangements designed for the advantage of men and women of one color or group or class, and for the exclusion of others. Nearly all countries have varying forms of discrimination against women, against minority religious communities, or against language groups.

What carries the label "human rights" in U.N. parlance is but a tiny fragment of the United Nations' potential relevance to discriminatory practices within its member countries. The work carried on under this banner has been mostly at the verbal level: the drafting of human rights conventions; U.N. seminars on human rights; the granting of fellowships for the study of civil rights law and procedures; conferences on criminal law, juvenile delinquency, and the treatment of offenders; special meetings on labor standards, women in political life, and other issues where the talk leads to more talk and not to international action programs.

In this whole area, the Kennedy and Johnson Administrations abandoned a ten-year-old tradition of American aloofness. U.S. delegations are now participating actively in the drafting of standard-setting recommendations and conventions in many fields of human rights. But the Senate has yet to consent to ratification of a single U.N. Human Rights Convention—not even the ones, on Forced Labor, Slavery, and Political Rights of Women, which raise no "states' rights" issues because they set international standards on clearly federal matters where U.S. practice is above the proposed universal standard. And no President has yet felt that these significant but essentially symbolic documents were worth major attention in a Senate already preoccupied with "must" legislation of absorbing interest to important groups of Americans.

Realistically, can the United Nations as an organization do something about the validation of our verbal values? Of course it can. It can switch on a floodlight, and expose the offending country and practice to the conscience of the world.

Let no one believe that this is a pointless exercise, unrelated to political reality. Under the strong light of world opinion, a nation's prestige is engaged; and since national power is not unrelated to national prestige, governments are influenced by world opinion—even though it is hard to prove because they seldom admit it. The blended conscience of men of good will may wink at injustice in the dark; but when the lights are on, a good conscience must speak, or desert its possessor. No government anywhere is immune to the moral indignation of those, including its own citizens, who watch it at work.

Right here is a policy question for us: As the necessary price for shining the U.N. searchlight on oppression elsewhere, are we Americans prepared to have the United Nations expose to embarrassingly public attention the skeletons hanging in our own closet?

The prospect does not fill me with alarm. Nothing the United Nations could do would much increase the candle power of public attention that already floods the scene wherever racial or religious discrimination is practiced by public agencies against the law, the Constitution, and the public policy of the United States. The United Nations is unlikely to reveal anything about America that is not already thoroughly in the public domain, by courtesy of our own political debates, our own wire services, and our own television networks.

No nation can wholly escape a roving international eye. But the maturing reaction of world opinion to Little Rock and Oxford and Birmingham and Selma demonstrates something very important: that even the most emotional drumbeaters for civil rights, thousands of miles from the scene, are quick to perceive the difference between a country which is having racial trouble because it is unwilling to make progress, and a country which is having racial trouble because it is getting on with an overdue job.

Surely the further development of this still primitive organization, to which we have given the presumptuous name "United

Nations," will feature a wider and more effective use of floodlight diplomacy. So here is an interesting and important question, like the problem of population policy, on which a certain amount of public discussion is a condition precedent to governmental courage.

The question is: How far should the United States urge the United Nations to go in holding its member nations to their human rights obligations under the Charter? Are there practical ways, consistent with the sovereign equality of nations (also a Charter principle), by which an international organization can protect and promote the rights and freedoms of individual men and women within their own national society, and even against their own government?

The question is not rhetorical, but real. No answer appears in the back of this book—or in the classified files of the State Department, either. And no far-reaching answer will be attempted inside our government, until there has been a great deal more discussion of the issue by the citizenry to which our government is responsible.

Fraternity
of the Impatient

10

Henri Bergson tells of a man in a parish church who remains impassive while, around him, the congregation is deeply moved by the pageantry of worship and the brilliance of the sermon. His neighbor in the pew asks him if he lacks all emotion and feeling, to remain thus unmoved, and the man replies: *"Mais, Monsieur, je ne suis pas de la paroisse."*

Luckily for mankind (we think), most Americans know that they are members of a parish of planetary size. As a people we are certainly moved to action by events in remote places. Nevertheless, we are still unaccustomed to our power, still doubters of our own prowess. Is it possible to build a world in which all peoples are safe because no one people is in charge? In world politics can we count, after all, on Jefferson's faith in "the genial influence of freedom"? I have illustrated at some length my own convictions that we are doing better than we think, and are capable of doing better than we know. Yet there remains this doubt that our democracy is equal to the task of combining with others to organize change and keep it peaceful.

Self-doubt in a free people is much older than our republic; it traces back to arguments among the ancient Greeks. In its American version we remember best the way it was put by Alexis de Tocqueville, who wrote so much so well about our fathers a century ago that only the very best speech writers are able to fashion a public address by a prominent American without some quote from *Democracy in America.*

"Foreign politics," said de Tocqueville, "demands scarcely any of those qualifications which are peculiar to a Democracy. They require, on the contrary, the perfect use of almost all those in which it is deficient."

"A Democracy," he added, "can only with great difficulty regulate the details of an important undertaking, persevere in a fixed design, and work out its execution in spite of serious obstacles. It cannot combine its measures with secrecy or await their consequences with patience."

De Tocqueville's famous foresight surely failed him here. Who is to say that the United States, which is without any doubt a democracy, has not been able to regulate the details of important undertakings, persevere in fixed designs, and work out their execution in spite of serious obstacles?

It *is* hard to combine our measures with secrecy. The curiosity of the American people, and the impressive technologies of their surrogates in the press, radio, and TV, have seen to that. I have suggested that the traditions of journalism do not always serve the public weal; the remedy, however, is not less journalism but better traditions. The greatest ally of a responsible foreign policy is certainly not an unattainable secrecy but the unrelenting attention of an understanding public.

De Tocqueville's most difficult hurdle is the last one. Can we await the consequences of our measures with patience? There is no doubt that this is hard work and requires rigorous training. But the record of twenty years—the recovery of Europe, the defense of the West, the liquidation of colonial rule, the beginnings of world economic development, the invention or adaptation of half a hundred international organizations, the vigor and dynamism of our own society—suggests that we and those with whom we have worked to "make the world safe for diversity" have on the whole lacked neither the courage to make big plans nor the persistence to bring them to fruition. In the end we outsmarted de Tocqueville: We made a virtue of impatience.

Yet the daily agony associated with these successes is enough to remind us that we have only begun to build the institutions to contain both the technology and the passions of man. The obstacles to international cooperation are everywhere to be seen, in walls of brick and steel, and in other barriers made of paper which limit the flow of people and goods across frontiers.

The rivalries and ambitions to which these walls bear witness can be policed by the application of enough power. Less force is required if it is wielded by international organizations, regional alliances, or the United Nations, which can substitute the mobilized conscience of world opinion for the actual employment of warriors and weapons—up to a point. Some rudimentary things we know about the policing of peace: how to arrange a cease-fire, how to patrol both sides of a tender frontier, how to repel aggression in the name of the world community, how to deter a nuclear threat in the name of civilization itself. But we are certainly better at cease-fires than at settlements. We know better how to keep a static lid on, than to contrive the changes that will make the peace-keeping lid unnecessary.

The big assignments are not the policeman's lot. They must be allotted to political leaders, especially the leadership of those nations which possess the power to act—the men, ships, planes, wheat, machine tools, computers, scientists, factories, technicians, and administrators that are the means and management of peaceful change.

As we look ahead to another twenty years of important undertakings, fixed designs, and politics of impatience, five tasks seem to require the special and urgent attention of American citizens, who ultimately tell their government how American power will and will not be employed.

One of these tasks is to work with our North Atlantic partners to accelerate, by deterrence and contagion, the evolution of a more responsible attitude by the Soviet Union toward world affairs. A second task is to prevent the proliferation of nuclear weapons. A third task is to teach the leadership of mainland China that aggression, naked or cloaked, does not pay. A fourth is to develop an enforceable ethic to govern intervention by the nations in each other's internal affairs. And a fifth is to develop the kinds of operational international agencies to which we can afford to entrust the common interest.

I have briefly traced in Chapter 3 the consequences of twenty years of effort to contain the Soviet Union. Viewed from the Kremlin balcony, neither the doctrines of Marx nor even the brilliant adaptations of Lenin seem to work very well. The Soviet empire is not expanding. Nuclear weapons turn out to be hard to use for blackmail. Soviet farm production is a disaster. And communism itself proves very difficult to sell because it is a divisive ideology, not a unifying one.

These results have been brought about partly by flaws in the Soviet system and partly by Western cohesion. The result is the more impressive when you consider how many and frequent are the exceptions to the solidarity of the West. The North Atlantic alliance built a system of military deterrence, capable of fighting a European aggressor in a small war, medium-sized war, or big war. The result has been no war at all, and a perceptible turn in the road for the Soviet Union. Feeling the pinch of their budget, fearing for the loyalty of their allies, figuring on greater returns through infiltration and aid in the developing countries outside Europe, the Russians decided in the early 1960s to freeze the mold of postwar Europe and see what could be done elsewhere to extend the area in which their writ might run.

The resulting stalemate looks like a *detente* to many Europeans, and some Americans. But anybody who gets a peek at what our intelligence services know about Soviet military technology is instantly cured of any temptation to euphoria. The Soviet government is investing large chunks of its controlled economy in developing, producing, and deploying the latest gadgets of advanced warfare. It is aiming medium range ballistic missiles at Western European targets, emplacing more intercontinental ballistic missiles in harder sites, working on an anti-missile missile, and constructing an impressive fleet of submarines and other instruments of naval warfare, supported by a global intelligence gathering network hidden in Soviet fishing fleets that operate in every ocean. Since 1961, when the U.N. registry was started, the Soviets have put nearly one hundred satellites into outer space (not counting failures) and most of them apparently for military purposes.

We can hardly object. Outer space and the high seas are free for peaceful uses (which include military uses if international law and the U.N. Charter are observed), and the Soviets' national budget is theirs to spend. Watching them as carefully as we can, we also are experimenting at the frontier of military technology, and believe that our imagination as well as our resources will continue to be more than a match for them. But we are doing this because we have to, faced as we are by an ideology which proclaims its desire to destroy diversity, in the service of a party that thinks it has a monopoly of truth and wishes it had a monopoly of power.

As long as dynamic technology is at the service of Communist politics, the rest of us have to maintain an effective deterrent at all levels of armed conflict which are in the range of Soviet capabilities. That does not require us to act as though the Soviets were about to jump us. We cannot know what they will do with their big modern armed forces. Therefore we and our allies must have the counterforce to handle them if the Soviet leaders place an aggressive intent behind their continuing military build-up. Malevolent intent without capability is not dangerous, but known capabilities with ambiguous intentions are not to be trifled with.

The success in deterring the Soviets in Europe has now produced a new set of problems there. Some of the Western Europeans are more relaxed now about the Soviet threat; they are impressed by the fact that the Soviets are mostly aiming their verbal barbs elsewhere (at the United States, at reactionary forces in the developing nations, and even at their sometime ally in Peking), and forget too easily that most of the Soviets' troops and weaponry are still aimed at Western Europe. At this writing, in the fall of 1965, the *detente* is a gossamer thing. You can see right through it to the unsolved problems of East-West relations. There is no move to settle the problems of a divided Germany or a divided Berlin, no stand-down of Soviet troops in Eastern Europe (perhaps because they distrust their own allies), and no active measure to slow down their Far Eastern allies.

Beyond the general relaxation born of prosperity and two decades of peace in Europe, there is the special problem of France. For seven years a Gaullist government has worked hard to detach itself from responsibility in the uncomfortable and demanding world outside Europe.

During the same seven years, the Fifth Republic has also been tackling an even harder task: It has been trying to detach itself from the future of Europe itself, by removing most of its forces from NATO, cutting down successive efforts to integrate the continental Six, and insisting on its own national nuclear force. As a consequence, the earlier hope that Europe would move quickly toward unity, and then work with the non-European members of NATO to build an Atlantic foreign policy, has been put off for years. Nonetheless, those Atlantic nations willing to work together must proceed to build the cohesion they need—harmonizing their trade and money policies, continuing to cooperate in defense arrangements including the nuclear variety, supporting Atlantic-wide research, development, and production schemes, "building bridges" to Eastern Europe, and working together in the United Nations to build a system of peaceful change in the turbulent world outside of Europe.

For the wisdom, leadership, imagination, and resources of Europeans are sorely needed to keep the free world well ahead of the Communists in science and technology, in military capabilities, and in practical influence around the world. Sharing the policeman's lot with our most natural allies will be a prime objective of American foreign policy for as far ahead as the Soviets are looking —and beyond, into that future the Chinese Communists hope is theirs.

After two decades of worrying about nuclear weapons, most informed people are more worried than ever today. And with reason. For the world is face to face now with a disturbing trauma.

Advanced science has made the instruments of murder and destruction so efficient that there is no general alternative to general peace. The big nuclear powers have learned, and the others will learn in time, that their inconceivable power could be used only in the presence of almost inconceivable provocation. President Johnson has underscored the point: "In a matter of moments, you can wipe out from 50 to 100 million of our adversaries, or they can in the same amount of time wipe out 50 million or 100 million of our people, taking half our land, taking half our population in a matter of an hour. So general war is impossible, and some alternatives are essential."

In the hands of two or three countries, the awesome force and enormous range of modern strategic weapons have made for a kind of stability. But now there are five members of the nuclear club, and a good many other nations are thinking about whether they can afford the initation fee. The prospect is that within the next few years half a dozen countries, or perhaps as many as ten or twelve, could develop their own nuclear weapons—and hand them to their friends. They have the scientists, the industry, and the imagination to do the job. Most of them presently lack the will and the incentive, but that could change. Nobody thinks this would make any sense, but it could happen. For there is no agreed machinery for making it unnecessary.

Ever since we offered to give our atomic weapons to the United Nations under the Baruch Plan, the United States has been looking for an agreed way to prevent the spread of such weapons around the world. The first decade and a half after the war featured a dialogue of the deaf, both in secret talks and in those amplified through the U.N. megaphone. Pragmatic U.S. plans for getting started on disarmament were answered with Soviet exhortations to sign first a treaty favoring a totally disarmed world. At the beginning of the Kennedy Administration we set forth our own picture of a world disarmed, one in which there were effective international organizations designed to keep the peace secure against secret arms and secret aggression. This settled the argument about general and complete disarmament by agreeing that everybody was for it, and made it possible to go to work on a few practical "next steps."

There has been a little progress: a ban on nuclear tests in the atmosphere, under water, and in outer space; the U.N. resolution against putting bombs in orbit; the "hot line" to reduce the danger of war by accident or miscalculation. But the nuclear arms race as a whole has not been turned down; it is still on the "up" escalator.

The Communists (minus China) and the West (minus France) have kept on working at disarmament because "world opinion," including their own, seems convinced that arms control must always be more important than it is discouraging. But meanwhile, technology is changing the subject. Mutual deterrence, described so vividly in Churchill's phrase about two scorpions in a bottle, made a general nuclear war seem unreal. Yet France and Communist China for different reasons began to advertise the notion that no nation was adult if it did not know how to split an atom in anger.

That the Chinese Communists and the French Gaullists poured resources and talent into building a bomb is sad, and might in the long run be dangerous. But the worst thing about these actions is that they are suggestive. India and Japan, naturally, are eyeing the change in Peking's blackmail potential. German politics has been deeply affected by General de Gaulle's notion that the primary basis for national pride is the ability to make and deliver megaton weapons.

The problem in the nuclear age is to achieve compliance by all nations with what the sheriff used to insist on at togetherness times in the Wild West: "Gents, please check your weapons at the door." That meant everybody except the law enforcement officials. It never was accepted practice for the good guys to leave their guns outside on a table if the bad guys were free to carry their pistols into the dance hall.

Four steps were involved: (1) agreement on the need for checking, (2) a place to check, (3) procedures to prevent cheating, and (4) effective ways to deal with anyone who cheated. A community which worked out ways to take these steps did not prevent quarrels and fights, much less greed and ambition and rivalry. But it did keep armed outbreaks to manageable proportions, and prevented much damage to innocent life, limb, and property. Today's world community is close to agreement on step (1), with public exceptions in Peking and Paris and hidden reservations in a good many other capitals. But the need for cheatproof checking has proved too high a hurdle because it brings into question the very maintenance of secret societies disguised as nations—or so the Communists believe.

The danger of nuclear spread is primarily a problem inside the free world. It would be good to have a Soviet assurance that they were not going to give other nations Soviet weapons or the means to make them. But the Soviets have shown little sign of interest in spreading their nuclear know-how. They got the Chinese started on the road to a bomb, but thought better of it by 1959. They do not even like to place their own nuclear weapons on the territory of their allies, as we have done in Europe.

The countries most liable to feel they must have at least a symbolic national weapon are China's neighbors, India and Japan; Pakistan, if India "goes nuclear"; Israel and the United Arab Republic, each escalating its weaponry in fear of the other; Sweden, to update the defense of its neutrality; and the Federal Republic of Germany. Some counsels in the United Kingdom, by contrast, call for submerging at least part of the modest British nuclear capability in some form of Atlantic force.

The practical approach to nuclear non-proliferation is therefore to find ways of calming the fears and meeting the legitimate needs of these specific nations which could, if they wished, exercise their sovereignty by making fission or even fusion warheads. The major powers, especially the free world's major power, cannot duck this issue, or even long postpone it, without an enormous increase in the instability of world politics. None of these nations can be made to withhold its resources from nuclear weapons production. But to start down that path is an expensive and dangerous decision; each of these nations, and others which might be tempted to add themselves to the list, might be induced to pool its security with the rest of us if we are wise enough to develop international security arrangements that give them a real voice in their own destiny.

The public hand-wringing and private head-scratching on disarmament and the proliferation of nuclear weapons will doubtless continue, and will be used by many nations for their own purposes. But beyond the sounds of public debate in the General Assembly and private talk at Geneva, there are the silent prayers of men and women who do not understand much about nuclear energy but know that they do not want their homes destroyed, their children burned alive, their hopes snuffed out by the miscalculated rivalries of political leaders. Here, in truth, is a problem beyond ideology—and for our own health and life we had better treat it with the urgency it deserves.

The detonation in 1965 of the first Chinese nuclear devices was only one evidence of a truculence which has become Peking's trademark in world affairs. The central problem in the Far East is the military and political behavior of the Chinese Communists—not, as some suppose, our military and political response to that behavior.

We are far from "ignoring" Communist China, as the recurrent debate on recognition and UN membership for Peking would suggest. Communist China is a geographic, demographic, and political fact of life which the United States government regularly takes into its calculations on a day-to-day basis. We ignore nothing about China which its policy of secrecy permits us to know.

It is quite fair, I think, to say that the Chinese Communists have carefully kept themselves at arm's length from the world community; and as part of that policy, they have kept themselves out of the United Nations. The United States, believing them unfit for civilized company under their present leadership, has willingly helped them stay out; and more than half the members of the U.N. General Assembly have consistently held the same view. But Mao Tse-tung and his colleagues have surely known for years that they could destroy most of the opposition to a U.N. seat for Peking by modifying their international behavior. They have, instead, attacked their neighbors and beaten the United Nations about the ears at every opportunity.

They hold it against the United Nations that it is trying to construct a system of peaceful change. They argue, as Stalin did, that war is the midwife of social change, the agent of destruction of an older order they desperately want to destroy. Latter-day Soviet prophets, beginning with Nikita Khrushchev, rationalized their way out of the doctrinal box when they realized that no nuclear power could afford to think of war as inevitable. Not so the men in Peking. They still stand where they stood. The dictum for which Mao Tse-tung will best be remembered, that "All political power grows out of the barrel of a gun," was repeated on the Peking radio in 1965.

Peace should be safeguarded, says Peking, not by relying on the United Nations but by "getting rid of intervention," not only in Korea but in the Congo, the Middle East, and Cyprus. The Chinese Communists even campaign against the humanitarian aid of the U.N. Specialized Agencies. On January 14, 1965, the Peking radio described such agencies as the Food and Agricultural Organization and the U.N. Children's Fund (UNICEF) as "serving U.S. purposes of interfering in the internal affairs of other countries . . . of U.S. economic and cultural aggression."

"In twenty years," the Chinese news service recently declared, ". . . the United Nations . . . has not done a single good deed. Instead it has a record replete with evil doings and crimes of aggression." Literature and rallies and broadcasts from Peking describe the United Nations officially as an "infamous organ," a "vile place," a "dirty stock exchange of international politics," and "an instrument of the world's rotting force."

The long and short of it is that the Chinese Communist leaders want no part of the United Nations as we know it—and the choice has been freely made. Indeed, Foreign Minister Chou En-lai told a 1965 rally that "another United Nations, a revolutionary one, may be set up so that rival dramas may be staged . . ."

Despite sentiments like these, close to half the governments that make up the United Nations now want the Peking leaders to take the China seat in the General Assembly. (Some of these think the Nationalist Chinese government on Formosa should also somehow retain an Assembly seat.) The most popular argument is that participation in U.N. work might help tame the Chinese Communists.

It is an enticing notion, for which evidence is wholly lacking. The men in Peking insist that nuclear testing is their own business, that they will "never" sign the test ban treaty, that they would not accept an invitation either to the Geneva Disarmament Conference or to five-power talks on nuclear disarmament: "We will not join such a club even if an invitation is sent to us on a silver platter."

We do not really have to speculate on the likelihood of the Chinese Communists moderating their doctrine in response to the feeling of others, or adjusting their behavior in the warm glow of cooperative enterprise, because this possibility already has been put sensationally to the test. Rather than yield on a point of dogma, rather than accommodate to the importunings of their greatest friend and closest ally, the Chinese Communist leaders have split the Communist monolith asunder, attempted to divide every Communist party in the world, given up massive economic and technical aid from the Soviet Union, and set back their own development perhaps by decades. If we need any instruction about the receptivity of the Chinese Communists to the influence of colleagues in a political club, we can learn all we need to know from the Soviet experience.

As things stand now, the idea of taming the current crop of Communist Chinese by exposure to the United Nations at work still belongs in the realm of mythology.

Peking has made enormous difficulties for her would-be friends in the United Nations. By loud talk and regional saber rattling, by remaining at war with the U.N. in Korea, threatening Formosa, supporting North Vietnam's attack on South Vietnam, subverting Cambodia, stirring up the Pathet Lao, threatening Thailand, invading India, and bristling at the Soviet Union, the Chinese Communists have greatly reduced the enthusiasm of delegates in the wings for the annual Chinese Representation item on the General Assembly agenda. The results in "world opinion" are curious: More people each year think the exclusion of Peking is silly, yet more nations have come to fear the influence of this obstreperous giant. They do not look forward to the day the Chinese enter the United Nations; they regard it as inevitable, but they fear it.

The Chinese Communists are obstreperous, but they are also careful. They have demonstrated in Korea and the Straits of Formosa that they, like the Soviets, know an impassable obstacle when they see one; they have shown in Assam and Ladakh that they can limit their warfare or even suspend it when it has served their purpose. At this writing they have refrained from direct intervention even in Vietnam, preferring so far to fight the United States to the last North Vietnamese.

Even a limited military success on our side might therefore persuade Hanoi and Peking that a true stalemate exists around the whole periphery of the Chinese land mass.

By unremitting military containment (representing mostly American effort at this stage) we could reach before long that stage of Mao's cyclical go-and-stop-then-go-again strategy when the light is turning amber and the force of politics is at least temporarily substituted for the politics of force. Once the Chinese Communists are stopped from "winning" in a military way—once they have learned that there is no further nourishment for the time being in militant violence beyond their frontiers—then they, like the Soviet leaders before them, will have to consider more flexible ways of pursuing their goals.

We shall have to be ready then both to make sure they remain militarily contained and to begin a long and probably tedious process of bargaining with them. The bargain to be struck is not with the United States, but between Peking and the organized world community. The two sides of the bargain will be simple in strategy, if complex in tactics: the Chinese Communists to progressively modify their behavior, in return for progressively greater opportunities to play a role in the community of nations that comports with the facts of their power and the requirements of their "face."

If this bargaining process is to serve the interests of a world of diversity, we had better widen to the maximum the community of those concerned with it. International peace-keepers, preferably mandated by the United Nations, should confirm and make routine the new rules of the Far Eastern game—which must be that the Chinese Communists "leave their neighbors alone." International "third men" should work to stabilize the Indian border, achieve internal peace in Vietnam and Laos, guarantee the safety of Formosa, negotiate a final settlement of Korea. Latent U.S. power will always have to be on tap to keep the bargain honest, but the power and influence of other nations should be brought into play. We have learned much about internationalizing police work and political mediation; we will need to apply all we have learned, and more, in the taming of the shrew in Peking. One of the main tasks for U.S. diplomacy in the years ahead is to help mobilize all nations that oppose the way Peking is using its power, in a strategy that trades acceptance of China for improvements in Chinese behavior.

To frustrate the ambitions of the more militant Far Eastern Communists and to contain such other political leaders as think they can get their way by the open threat or covert use of arms, we are going to need international force in the service of international law.

The U.N. Charter contains plenty of law for the purpose. But we would do well to have a sharp look at the ragged regulations around which we are building world order. The structure of peace depends heavily on the ambiguous rule that each nation will respect the nationhood of others, and will not intervene in its internal affairs. That structure still precariously stands, but the termites are gnawing at its foundations.

The principle in its pure form is no longer a useful guide to behavior. For the central fact about modern international relations is that nations are deeply and permanently enmeshed in each other's internal affairs. They are involved through aid programs and military training and fellowships for students and leaders; through the beneficent dispatch of culture and the acrimonious exchange of propaganda; through a thousand pluralistic channels ranging from trade unions to the Red Cross.

In Asia, Africa, and Latin America, nearly every country wants and needs the help of outsiders in achieving those "better standards of life in larger freedom" that are the goal of their aspirations and the promise of their independence. Outsiders are therefore bound to be involved to some extent in their essentially domestic affairs.

Under what restraints will the outsiders operate on the inside? When the question comes up, we tell ourselves that intervention is all right as long as the government of the receiving country asks the foreigner to come and permits him to stay.

That rough-and-ready ethic of intervention seems to work rather well for the control of overt outsiders. It even seems to have caught and held the respectful attention of aggressors. Most nations have come to believe now that it is unfashionable to raise a flag, roll the drums, and march in daylight across an international demarcation line onto the territory of another nation. India's take-over of Goa and then its 1965 action against Pakistan—retaliating, to be sure, for the secret infiltration of several thousand Pakistani in Kashmir—are almost the only exceptions to the rule in recent years.

Now if you consider the story of man from the beginning of things, the more or less effective outlawing of formal, advertised aggression is no mean accomplishment. If there is a strong presumption against overt military operations in somebody else's country, that is certainly one up for the progress of civilization.

But the very fact that formal invasions are out of fashion has led to widespread adoption of a new practice: hidden intervention by nations in the internal politics of their neighbors, including the financing, equipping, and manning of rebel forces seeking power by violent means. Most of the fighting and killing that now goes on in Asia, Africa, and Latin America can be traced to outside interventions, playing on local rivalries to overthrow governments by ostensibly indigenous means.

If the principle is established that the outsiders, not the insiders, decide when intervention is all right, the fragile fabric of nationhood will come apart at the seams in dozens of newly independent nations. Every nation has its dissidents, its internal struggle for power, its domestic arguments about who is going to be in charge and how the country should be run. But if every internal rivalry is to become a Spanish Civil War, with each faction drawing in armed friends from nearby and great powers from far away, the history of nationalism will be written in blood and shame throughout Africa and Asia in this century. (This was, for example, the issue in the brief but spectacular "hostage snatch" in the Congo, where Belgian troops ferried by the U.S. Air Force rescued people who were being held for political blackmail by Congolese rebels in Stanleyville. The hostages were removed by permission of the Congo's legitimate government. The Stanleyville rebels were being aided by several African nations without any such permission.)

The "law" that outsiders should be invited, not crash the party, is far from a clear prescription. Invitations can be forged, and the government officials who issue them can be bribed or seduced. Who can forget the "request" from the Kadar government for the Russian tanks that crushed the freedom fighters in Hungary? But still, the principle of permission is the best ethic mankind has yet developed to prevent a reversion to imperialism and foreign domination. And its durability is proved by the very lengths to which the perpetrators of "wars of liberation" go to create phony local authorities by whom the ambitious outsiders can claim they were "invited."

The useful if subvertible principle of permission is also hard to apply when there are no legitimate authorities to issue or withhold an invitation. The "law" as it stands assumes a functioning government covering every piece of the world's real estate. But in the Dominican Republic on April 28, 1965, and for several months thereafter, no government credibly existed. President Johnson actually had in hand an "invitation" from a military group claiming to be the government. But to avoid recognizing its rather moldy claim, the President ordered the Marines ashore on his own judgment that mass killing would result if he did not act. Soon thereafter, the OAS took jurisdiction of the philosophical problems involved, certified the absence of effective local authority, and regularized the presence of American (and later other hemispheric) troops. But for a short time the ultimate restraint on the outsiders' action was in the hands of a single outsider—*faute de mieux*.

The growing trouble over indirect interventions in Asia and Africa points to the need for effective international regulation of the mutual and often necessary involvement of the nations in each other's affairs. Durable laws and limits can be set only by the action, or inaction, of international organizations. In the post-colonial world of diversity, no nation can assert a general right on its own initiative to take charge of other people's destinies. That is why our every national action, in every crisis, has to be taken in full awareness of its implications for the relevant regional organization and for the United Nations; the institutions of peace will wither or grow according to whether they are bypassed or put to work each time the peace is broken.

The cue for U.S. policy is, of course, to see that they are put to work. If we do, the duty of policing the principle of non-intervention can be widely shared. But to the extent that international organizations are not up to the job of keeping the peace and mediating change, the United States as residual peace-keeper will find each dispute in its own reluctant lap. We know from experience in Vietnam and elsewhere that when we must ourselves defend a small country against disguised intervention, it is a painful and expensive task indeed. The only course more painful and more expensive would be to ratify by inaction the principle that intervention is permissible if the intervener denies he is intervening.

To convert the Soviet Union to peaceful cooperation, to prevent or regulate the spread of nuclear weapons, to tame the Far Eastern Communists, to codify and enforce an ethic of mutual intervention —these global chores will excite our emotions and occupy our minds for many years to come. I have touched in prior chapters on other issues that also will require our attention and our resources, such as the growing gap between the richest countries and the poorest countries, the need for some regulation of population growth, the problem of building the institutions of cooperation to match the "thundering impact of discovery."

The politics of peace-keeping is not inherently more important than the arithmetic and administration of economic and social development. But the peace cannot be built if it cannot be kept. We have just learned how to destroy the world, so the regulation of men's passions has become a simple necessity: There must be no more war. But we have also just established the principle that every people will manage its own destiny and be master of its own passions. If the world community cannot develop a way to regulate these passions—if, in short, the world cannot become a community—then the danger of extinction is a literal possibility in our time.

The smell of this danger is most clearly evident these days in the loosening of civilized restraints on international behavior.

In June of 1950, when I was working for Paul Hoffman in the Marshall Plan, I had to substitute for him in making a speech at Colgate University. Remembering Burke's commentary on the turbulence of his time, I called this speech "Reflections on the Revolution of Rising Expectations." The phrase has since been attributed to a good many other people (who are more than welcome to it), but I think this was the first time it saw the light of day.

In the decade and a half since then, those rising expectations have swept across the colonial world and doubled the count of national sovereignties. Men and women who fifteen years ago were students or revolutionaries, or both, are today in charge of their countries' governments—or have already given way to younger students and more effective revolutionaries.

The aspirations that have risen so fast were well described in the U.N. Charter as "better standards of life in larger freedom." How the passions of our time have been aroused by passionate versions of that sober and balanced phrase! The ugly book burnings in Europe a generation ago are matched now by the burning of libraries elsewhere as a political gesture. When responsible governments organize or permit mobs in their own streets to attack foreign embassies, we are witnessing not just the breakdown of diplomatic niceties but an uglier process in which racial and national emotion breaks through the fragile crust of civilization itself.

Nationhood is heady stuff. Every nation and every national leader can be expected to overindulge once in a while. But continued overindulgence in nationalist emotion can lead to much senseless killing. It is surely time, as Pope Paul VI has said, to "raise a dike" against the passions of men, for they threaten to swallow up in indignities what Paul's predecessor, John XXIII, kept calling the "natural dignity" of individual men and women.

The essential question about the international institutions we need to build for peace-keeping and peace building is this: Will the peoples of 120 nations, and especially their leaders, graduate fast enough from the "revolution of rising expectations" to the "evolution of rising responsibility"?

The need for a rising standard of responsibility is most evident in the United Nations, because the United Nations is a magnified mirror of the tensions and rivalries and dilemmas in the real world. The U.N. General Assembly started twenty years ago with fifty-one members. Even then the United States did not always have its way in the U.N., but the pre-eminence of U.S. leadership was seldom in question among the men and women, some of them great men and women, who came to the U.N. from every continent. Now the United Nations has 117 members, and it will probably grow past 125. Most of its formal actions still, miraculously, are consistent with the vital interests of the United States—because our true interest is so often the common interest. But the politics of U.N. leadership is vastly more complicated now, and each year puts a more severe strain on American skill and American nerves.

Two-thirds of the votes in the General Assembly now represent less than 5 per cent of the contributions to the organization. Large majorities are now available to pass resolutions telling the nuclear powers how to disarm, the big trading nations how to liberalize their commercial policies, and the rich countries how to spend their money. The leaders of the smaller and poorer countries are loud in their impatience with the existing order of things; they expect the United Nations and its agencies to change the world, and in a hurry. But most of them still put more faith in large parliamentary majorities at public sessions than in mutual persuasion through quiet diplomacy.

Now that the net recipients of aid from the U.N. system have more than two-thirds of the votes in the specialized "legislatures" of the world community, they have quite naturally organized to bargain collectively with the contributors—and brought into being a contributors' caucus to bargain collectively with them. The result is a growing amount of public debate in which the poor countries say out loud that the rich men's world owes them a living, and the richer countries reply that they can only help effectively if the poor countries do a number of things inside their own countries to make foreign aid effective. At the end of these debates, votes are sometimes taken which reflect the parliamentary situation but make a nonsense of the situation in the real world.

In UNESCO (the United Nations Educational, Scientific, and Cultural Organization, with headquarters in Paris), a budget vote in 1964 found countries representing two-thirds of the contributions voting *against* the budget which was then duly adopted. At the first U.N. Conference on Trade and Development, large majorities passed resolutions recommending changes in the commercial policies of nations holding a minority of the votes in the conference, but representing about three-quarters of world trade. The problem was perceptively stated by a thoughtful delegate from the Philippines. "It is an obvious fact," he said, "that on the basis of simple majority, the developing nations can outvote the developed nations at any time. Yet, what will it avail this conference to reach decisions by simple majority if the defeated minority includes the very countries from whom concessions are expected?"

There is, I believe, a real danger that the coinage of the United Nations will be debased by premature votes on one-sided propositions. The engineers who deal with complex physical systems have coined a phrase we might find a use for in the U.N. system. When one of the vital parts gives an input to the total machine more powerful than the machine's feedback system can correct, the machine goes into a state they call "runaway to maximum." It results in a kind of nervous breakdown of the machine. If the corrective feedback processes already built into the U.N. system do not operate effectively, there is real danger of a "runaway to maximum" that will disrupt the intimate cooperation on which peace and growth both depend.

Debates in which the industrialized countries attribute the world's troubles to the developing countries, and the developing countries in turn attribute their troubles to "colonialists," will be worse than useless. But something useful can and will happen in the U.N. machinery if, so to speak, we all leave the rostrum, move together to the workbench, and there together address ourselves to building a serious system of world order and conducting a massive war on poverty.

Those of us who achieved the envied status of "industrialized nations" relatively early cannot in good conscience resent the impatience of the U.N. majority for national security, better life, and larger freedom. On the contrary we not only honor and applaud the impatience of the developing countries—we share it. Welcome to the fraternity of the impatient, we say. We too wish to disarm. We too wish to move faster in the development effort. We too wish to build international agencies to lubricate the channels of international cooperation. For two decades past, we Americans have been insistently and impatiently proposing arms control, supporting international peace-keeping, deterring and resisting threats to the peace, and pushing economic and social development—in the face of enormous obstacles of ideology, tradition, and apathy. We have spent $800 billion on the defense of the free world and provided more than 40 billions of public dollars for capital investment around the world, to bear witness to our impatience with the needless dangers of the arms race, the still tiny capacity of the United Nations for peace-keeping, and the sluggish pace of economic growth and social progress in most of the nations of the world.

So let us join, we say, in using our common impatience to speed the solution of these common problems of peace-keeping and development, rather than merely using it on each other.

A situation in which all nations are juridically equal, but some are practically more equal than others, creates a constitutional dilemma which is or ought to be familiar to citizens of the United States of America. Our ancestors worked themselves out of that problem in our own U.S. Constitution by using bicameralism: one House of Congress would represent states, the other would represent population.

In the United Nations a similar great compromise is in the making. The Security Council, where the great powers are permanently represented, will normally be the first port of call in peace and security questions. The General Assembly, where each nation regardless of size has one vote, can discuss and resolve on symbolic matters; but when it comes to action the Assembly can only recommend, not tell its members to act.

The issue that posed the constitutional question was the fight in 1964 and 1965 over whether the Soviet Union and France, which had been assessed by the General Assembly for the U.N. peace-keeping operations, would have to pay up or (under Article 19 of the Charter) lose their Assembly votes. After a long struggle, the small-country majority of the Assembly was clearly unwilling to fight for its most important Charter power, the power to charge the U.N.'s operations to all its members.

The fact that the United Nations will not now use the "every-member canvass" to finance its major operations does not mean it can do less; it may, paradoxically, enable it to do more peace-keeping, sooner and on a larger scale.

The reason is plain. Getting everybody to participate in U.N. operations is possible only at the cost of drastically limiting the size and scope of the operations, and at the further cost of limiting such operations to those which the Soviets are prepared to back. Since the United States as residual peace-keeper may have to pick up most of the pieces, and most of the checks, which are not picked up by international organizations, it is *not* in the U.S. national interest thus to limit the potential of the United Nations as an operational agency in the peace-keeping and development fields.

There are two additional advantages, from the point of view of the U.S. interest in the United Nations, in a voluntary system by which U.N. operations are normally financed—and managed—by consortia of those members willing and able to undertake collective operations under the U.N. flag.

One advantage is negative. There is always the possibility that the small-country majority in the United Nations might irresponsibly decide to "soak the rich" by charging an unfair share of peace-keeping operations to a few big countries, or by setting up a soft and expensive Capital Development Fund. Now that the Assembly has made clear that it is not prepared to enforce its own assessment power, the "possible horrible" of our having to pay for a U.N. operation to which we fundamentally object can be dropped from our domestic political nightmares.

The other advantage is more positive. Over the years ahead we will be continuously bargaining with the net recipients of benefits from the U.N. system about the size and content of budgets for operational activities by the U.N. and the various agencies of the "U.N. family." If the principle is established that major U.N. operations are normally financed on a voluntary basis, the bargaining power of the larger contributors at the budget tables will of course be enhanced.

Yet it is not in the U.S. interest to destroy the Charter principle, which is still that all members can be taxed by action of all members, and that they must pay these taxes or lose their vote in the General Assembly. We Americans have our experience with the 14th and 15th Amendments to our Constitution, which were adopted and ratified a century before the political consensus was available to enforce throughout our nation their strictures against government-sponsored racial discrimination. It was surely better to keep that law on our books, even while it was not being enforced, precisely to hasten the day of its enforcement.

In the same way, it is wise now to preserve in the U.N. system the noble idea that international action for peace is the national obligation of every government member of the United Nations—even if we cannot yet depend on two of the permanent members of the Security Council (the USSR and France), or more than about half of the smaller countries, to support in tangible ways the use of U.N. peace-keeping machinery in an emergency.

Our destiny would be safer if the progress of civilization were now farther along—if the Cold War were less divisive, and if the small countries were more acutely aware of the financial and political cost of nationhood. Eventually, as the young countries shake off their timidity and if the Cold War thaws, it may be possible to secure worldwide support for worldwide operations. When that day comes, it would be better to have "collective financial responsibility" still enshrined in the Charter; otherwise, the every-member principle will then have to be invented and negotiated all over again.

It would be nice if it had not turned out that the Founding Fathers of the United Nations in 1945 were still ahead of their time in 1965. But in international politics, as in the domestic variety, we always have to start from where we are, not from where it would be nice to be. Starting from here, we still can, should, and must develop the world institutions to cope with a world of small wars and nuclear dangers, in which both the peril and the promise are increasingly global.

Those who are kept awake by fear and feelings of pessimism—by the rich-poor gap, the Soviet enigma, the nuclear danger, the Chinese threat, the multiple interventions of nations in each other's affairs, and the swirling majorities of the world community—might take comfort from an entry Samuel Pepys made in his diary 300 years ago:

"Great talk among people how some of the Fanatiques do say that the end of the world is at hand, and that next Tuesday is to be the day. Against which, whenever it shall be, good God, fit us all!"

We Americans are uncomfortable in the presence of fanatics, and do not believe that "next Tuesday is to be the day." We are allied with forty-two nations, spend $50 billion a year on defense, and support the United Nations precisely to make sure that the end of the world is indefinitely postponed.

Whether we succeed depends partly on others, but mostly on ourselves. We might well prefer to be less bothered by responsibility, less distracted by the brickbats that are the price of power, less burdened by the need to understand others which is the price of peace. But if a world system of peaceful change is going to be built, we of all people cannot afford to be less committed to the project than we are.

For a brief period of my life I was a teacher—the easiest job to do badly, and the most difficult of all jobs to do well. While writing and rewriting the words in this book, I have tried to think what I would be trying to teach American youngsters about world affairs if I were back at teaching now. There are seven things I think I would ask them to learn and keep in their minds as they grow up, citizens of the world's greatest power—which has to mean responsible citizens of the world's most responsible power.

• *Learn to love diversity.* All men are brothers, but all brothers are different. No nation, no doctrine, no culture will conquer this planet. Our world, thank God, is and will remain pluralistic—and for this reason colorful and interesting and exciting to live in.

• *Learn to beware of labels and categories.* No society in this world bears any real resemblance to communist society as seen by Karl Marx, or to capitalist society as understood by Adam Smith. The struggles we see are never clear if they are viewed as simple, and never simple once they are clear.

• *Learn to choose between sharply different shades of grey.* There is a real difference between aggressor and defender in armed conflict, even if the defender is not quite a saint. If there were nothing to choose between the major protagonists in the so-called Cold War, then the whole of postwar history would make no sense at all.

• *Learn to watch the deeper trends of world events.* The surface is subject to quick storms and sudden calms, neither of which tells us much of tomorrow's weather. So keep a close eye on the main streams and on the quiet, lesser currents—how strong and how fast they flow, and where and when they promise to converge or to veer apart.

• *Learn that power is a many-sided thing, to be used with great care.* Power is wealth and armed strength; but it is also fine deeds and great expectations and warm feelings—and it rests at least partly upon good example. Great power is inseparable from great responsibility; and in many ways the mightiest nation in the world community is the most involved with all other nations. The action we take together had better contain the peril we share, for we all have to be brothers whether we like it or not.

• *Learn not to worry too much about what other people say.* To prove their independence, which we want them to have, they sometimes have to thumb their noses at those who have the power to act for peace. But fortunately, the basis for our self-esteem and the measure of success in our foreign policy are not gratitude or popularity, but respect and results.

• *Learn to enlighten your judgment with a healthy touch of optimism.* Time and change alter the contours of every dispute. The problem is never as big as the biggest expert thinks it is. And man always has in him something more, and something better, than appears at the moment.

These and other nuggets of distilled experience only confirm what instinct and freedom and faith and preference tell us in our bones: The wave of the future is still the open society—and the engine of that society is still the open mind of the free individual.

Index

Born in New York City in 1918, HARLAN CLEVELAND was graduated from Andover and Princeton, followed by a Rhodes Scholarship at Oxford in 1938–1939. Since then he has worked successfully at three careers—government administrator, editor and publisher, and graduate school dean—and is working at a fourth career as diplomat and statesman.

For a dozen years he managed foreign economic programs for the U.S. government, including postwar stints as an aid administrator for the U.N. in Italy and China. Then he left Washington to become executive editor, and later publisher, of the *Reporter*. In 1956 he was appointed dean of the Maxwell Graduate School of Citizenship and Public Affairs at Syracuse University. In 1961 President Kennedy brought him back to Washington as assistant secretary of state for International Organization Affairs, and in 1965 President Johnson appointed him U.S. ambassador to NATO. He has written or edited six books and is the author of numerous articles.

Ambassador Cleveland is still on leave as professor of political science at Syracuse. Since his appointment to NATO, he and his wife live in Paris with one of their three children; the other two attend college in America.